THE HEART OF AN ANGEL

BECOMING GOD'S MESSENGERS OF LOVE AND HOSPITALITY TO A WORLD IN NEED!

THE HEART OF AN ANGEL

BECOMING GOD'S MESSENGERS OF LOVE AND HOSPITALITY TO A WORLD IN NEED!

TOM ENGLISH AND WILMA ESPAILLAT ENGLISH

AN IMPRINT OF DEAD LETTER PRESS
BOX 134, NEW KENT, VA 23124-0134

The Heart of an Angel
First published 2016 by Ravens' Reads
An imprint of
DEAD LETTER PRESS

This edition © 2016

Printed in the United States of America

ISBN-10: 0-9966936-1-0
ISBN-13: 978-0-9966936-1-5

FIRST EDITION
May 3, 2016

DEAD LETTER PRESS
BOX 134, NEW KENT, VIRGINIA 23124-0134
WWW.DEADLETTERPRESS.COM

This book is
lovingly dedicated to

Ruth Lillian Carreras Espaillat

and

Wanda Espaillat

True servants and messengers of God's love;
Two "angels"—like those described herein
—who continue to abundantly bless our lives.

God is not unjust; He will not forget your work
and the love you have shown Him as you have
helped His people and continue to help them.
—Hebrews 6:10 NIV

CONTENTS:

INTRODUCTION:
BAND OF ANGELS!

After [Jesus] had fasted forty days and forty nights, He was hungry. ...And immediately angels came and began to serve Him.

—Matthew 4:2, 11 (Holman CSB)

THROUGHOUT BIBLICAL TIMES GOD used an army of celestial beings to make special announcements, and to minister to His people on earth. These supernatural beings frequently visited our mortal world in the guise of strangers traveling along the dusty byways of life.

God's Heavenly Messengers are universally known today as *angels*. But in a manner of speaking, we're all God's "Heavenly Messengers" here on earth: we all have a story to tell, an experience to relate, a testimony to share; and, like His celestial band of servants, the Creator of the Universe wants each of us to be a Godly emissary of His supernatural love. He wants each of us to follow in the footsteps of His Son Jesus Christ, through a lifestyle of giving, serving, encouraging, and ... sharing the Words of Life!

Couple this truth with the knowledge that God created each of us in His own image—thus placing within our hearts a precious spark of the divine—and it's easy to conclude that ... in a manner of speaking ... we are all God's angels in this life!

If this seems like a novel view of *who* we are—or *should* be—and *what* we're about, it's not! If we truly believe in the God of Abraham, Isaac and Israel, and seek to do His will in all things, then this poetic analogy perfectly reflects both our spiritual identity and our ultimate purpose in this hectic world. Trust us, this "shoe" comes in one size only, but it actually fits everyone!

God, however, desires much more than a clever analogy. He's been calling His people to actually *do* the work of the angels since the beginning of time! We've just missed it. Or should we say, *strayed* a bit from the truth? Fortunately, it's never too late (or too soon) to rediscover a lost truth. And our Lord always manages to gather together His flock, no matter how far we roam!

God is calling His flock to once again embrace its *angelic* role to a world in need. He's actively recruiting these days, looking for faithful servants who are ready to join His band of angels. But do *you* have what it takes?

You do! We all do! But in order to fly with the angels, we'll need to go through some basic training. Call it boot camp for angels—except there's no drill sergeant. And consider this humble little book the official training manual. It won't teach you how to pitch a tent, dig a foxhole, or light a campfire, but it does explain what it takes to develop the "heart of an angel"!

The *heart* of an angel describes the loving, welcoming, and accepting disposition and habits God longs to cultivate in each of us. It's not something that comes naturally, but there are a few *basic* things we can do to facilitate our own growth, all of which we share within. This angelic heart is also strengthened and characterized by a *simple* approach to social interaction which was instituted by God Himself. And while this approach may at first seem an unimportant "side issue," it's anything but. It's the single most important "ministry" of the angels!

The true heart of an angel is distinguished by a lifestyle of *hospitality!*

● STOP! ●

If you think you already know *everything* about Biblical Hospitality, then you probably don't know nearly enough. And if you think the practice of hospitality is not something you're personally called to—no matter what the reasons—then you *need* this book.

To begin with, the practice of hospitality is actually a sacred command for *everyone!* And yet, it's one of the most neglected and misunderstood Biblical concepts today! For instance, it's NOT the same thing as Modern entertaining, and it's NOT for women only!

Hospitality not only characterizes the heart of an angel, but it's also the purest expression of the divine nature and character of the Creator of the Universe! After all, the God of the Bible is first and foremost a *hospitable* God. But when was the last time you heard anyone refer to Him in this way?

With *The Heart of an Angel*, we hope to set the record straight regarding the practice of hospitality, while bringing clarity to several key issues facing our churches and communities.

In the pages that follow, we define God's original concept for social interaction, based on numerous scriptural references, as well as the examples of key

Biblical figures. We also explain how the practice of hospitality impacts every area of our lives, and why it's vital to the spiritual, emotional, and physical health of our families, friends, coworkers, and even people we've yet to meet!

We'll dispel several myths surrounding hospitality, which have resulted in the neglect of the practice—to the detriment of both our civil and faith communities. We'll explain how hospitality significantly differs from the art of entertaining, a secular pursuit that's had many unintended and unfortunate consequences on God's people and the world at large.

Along the way, we'll visit with the great Biblical Patriarch Abraham. We'll recount his history-making encounter with the supernatural, and learn how the event changed the destiny of all humankind. And while many know him as "The Father of Faith," we'll show you why he's the icon of yet *another* spiritual attribute, and explain how these attributes work hand-in-hand.

We'll explore the pitfalls of modern entertaining, and then meet two very different "angels" named Martha! We'll learn what God Himself expects from a good host or hostess, and examine the "one thing" that makes God feel truly welcome—in both your heart and home.

We'll explain why "hospitality starts at home," and then tell you how to make that home a refuge of refreshing and restoration, a place where God will show up to work miracles. We'll even let you in on a few "secrets" only the angels understand!

We hope to inspire and encourage you to fly to new heights, while giving you plenty of new insights to think about. And maybe here and there we'll even be able to supply you with a good laugh! But, more than anything else, we want you to understand what it takes to have the heart of an angel, and why GOD WANTS YOU!—and needs you!

Join us in this great endeavor, and learn how you, too, can be a part of God's band of angels!

Tom English
Wilma Espaillat English
New Kent, VA

ABOUT THE AUTHORS:

Wilma Espaillat English *grew up in a bilingual, bicultural family in New York and New Jersey, learning firsthand the significance of hospitality in the Hispanic culture. Today she is a published writer, speaker and educator. She has taught a variety of subjects including Business English, Public Speaking, Spanish, and Ancient World History, at both high school and college levels. She has written high school curriculum for classes in Multicultural Studies, and conducted seminars for civic groups, including law enforcement agencies. She's also taught Bible and Christian Life topics to adults ranging in age from 18 to 80. She's the wife of Tom English.*

Tom English *grew up in a "Southern fried" family in rural Virginia. Today he is a Senior Chemist at Newport News Shipbuilding. He is also a published writer and an award-nominated editor of both fiction and nonfiction. Most recently, his fantasy-adventure fiction has appeared in the print anthologies* Challenger Unbound *and* Gaslight Arcanum: Uncanny Tales of Sherlock Holmes. *Tom also edited the mammoth* Bound for Evil: Curious Tales of Books Gone Bad, *a 2008 Shirley Jackson Award finalist for best anthology. Like* *his wife, Wilma, he has extensive knowledge in Biblical Studies and has taught many Christian Life classes to singles and "young" married couples ages 18 to 80. He resides with Wilma, surrounded by books and beasts, deep in the woods of New Kent, Virginia.*

Tom and Wilma invite you to join them each weekday for humorous and inspiring new articles at their internet home, www.AngelAtTheDoor.com

Also available from Ravens' Reads:
DIET FOR DREAMERS: INSPIRATION TO FEED YOUR DREAMS, ENCOURAGEMENT TO FOSTER YOUR CREATIVITY!

ANGEL IN THE KITCHEN: TRUTH & WISDOM INSPIRED BY FOOD, COOKING, KITCHEN TOOLS AND APPLIANCES

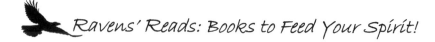
Ravens' Reads: Books to Feed Your Spirit!

CHAPTER 1:
TOUCHED BY AN ANGEL!

FOR DECADES THE ENTERTAINMENT INDUSTRY has demonstrated its fascination with angelic beings. Literary thrillers have introduced them into several controversial and pretty farfetched novels, all to service their doctrinally incorrect plots; and big-budget movies have used every CGI trick in the business to help audiences to "see" these supernatural creatures. But despite all the special effects at their disposal, and despite all the "pseudo-facts" employed by writers, both Hollywood and pop culture have failed at depicting the most vital aspect of God's "secret agents."

Few of these works of fiction have allowed us to catch a glimpse of the heart of an angel! And believe it or not, in real life, it's not that hard to see! In fact, we plan to explore the hidden hearts of angels in the pages that follow, and bring a new perspective to a familiar debate: do angels still operate in the world today? The answer may surprise you!

One iconic piece of pop culture that did manage to capture the true nature of these supernatural beings

7

was the hit television series *Touched by an Angel*, which premiered in 1994, and ran for nine seasons or 211 episodes. Each week the show's two angels, amiably played by Della Reese and Roma Downey, would receive their latest assignment straight from God—which was theologically correct and entirely fitting.[1] After all, as angels, these two special agents are servants of God, sent to earth by Him to help humans with various problems and issues.

In the course of performing their divine duties, these angels would assist people facing difficult times. They might help an alcoholic sober up; find a home for an orphan or a street person; comfort a disabled vet; encourage a dreamer to fulfill a goal; prompt a selfish and materialistic businessman to re-evaluate what's important in life; reunite estranged family members; and, in general, urge their flawed human "assignments" to accept those who are ethnically and socially different, to show compassion for the poor and needy, to forgive people who had wronged them, to reconnect and rebuild relationships, and ultimately to draw closer to God.

By the end of every episode, these wonderful angels faithfully completed their "secret mission." Usually they did so in spite of seemingly impossible odds, and after overcoming incredible obstacles. Nevertheless, they always managed to help their human friends in need— the people God created in His own image—to be all that they *could* be!

Throughout the entire run of this encouraging series, one thing remained constant: the angels always made a positive contribution to the lives of the people they encountered, particularly in the area of human

---

[1] For more information on Biblical Angels, please refer to the Supplement: God's Supernatural Messengers, on page 189.

relationships. Actually, these agents of God continually left the men, women and children they were assigned better off than when they found them! Hence, the people they encountered knew they'd been "touched by an angel"!

Each of us has the potential to similarly touch the lives of the people we meet. With God's help, we can have a positive impact on friends, family, coworkers ... and even strangers! And we can make a real difference in our homes and communities—*if* we're willing to accept the assignment God wants each and every one of us to accomplish! What's our mission? It may sound a little impossible, but it's not: God simply wants all of us to be His "angels"!

Don't laugh, because the word *angel* comes from the Latin term *angelos*, meaning "messenger"; and God's supernatural agents are precisely that, delivering good tidings and words of encouragement to those in need. But then, don't we *all* have a message to share? In essence, God intends our very lives to send a message to the world. Each of us was created to be His "living letter" to those we meet. (2 Corinthians 3:3) So, in a spiritual sense, we're all messengers. However, the analogy doesn't end here.

People are as unique as their DNA; no two are alike. Furthermore, each of us is the product of our upbringing, our national origin and our ethnicity. Each of us comes from a unique background, with unique experiences. We are all one-of-a-kind masterpieces created by God, and every last one of us can declare with the Psalmist, King David, "Thank you for making me so wonderfully complex! Your workmanship is marvelous!" (Psalm 139:14 NLT)

While we're on the subject, we'll point out that we didn't use the term *race* in the above paragraph. What people generally define as *race* should never differentiate us, and we've personally decided to jettison the word —because we're all members of a single race, the *human* race. We were all created in God's own image, and we're all descended from a single bloodline. (Genesis 1:26) But thank goodness we're not all the same! Our uniqueness and individual "flavor" derives from a variety of cultures, ethnicities and backgrounds. God loves diversity—just take a look at nature and you'll understand this—and when He created the human race He seasoned the world with a wide variety of "flavors"! Or, as Hispanics would say, *¡Sabor!*

Our life experiences, particularly our spiritual journeys, as well as other factors such as education (both formal and informal), gives each of us a distinctive perspective on life. We all have something to share, something special to bring to the table. Each of us has a unique voice and a personal message to deliver. Question is, exactly what type of message are we sending?

Ever hear someone say, "You're sending the wrong message"? Unfortunately, God may have good cause to say the same thing about many of us. At times we *act* and *react* in selfish, self-centered, and shameful ways, saying things we usually regret as soon the words spew from our mouths; but God wants each of us to carry instead a *Godly* message that impacts lives in a way that leaves people feeling as though they were "touched by an angel"!

God wants all the members of His "family" to be *angelic* messengers of love, hope and truth. In essence, He wants us to be the messengers of an ancient and universal practice that has endured the test of time, a sacred charge capable of transforming lives, a divine duty called ... *Oops!* We're getting a little ahead of ourselves.

To become God's "supernatural" messengers, we must first allow God to speak to us and to have free rein in every area of our lives. We must ask Him to give us the heart of an angel!

The heart of an angel can be described with a single word, HOSPITABLE! This one word says it all: loving, accepting, welcoming. Hospitable people open their hearts and homes to others; they are sensitive to the needs of those around them; they make room in their lives for the people they meet. Oh yeah, and they continually practice the Biblical (and generally misunderstood) concept of hospitality!

Hospitality is ... probably not even close to what you *think* it is! In actuality, it's like an onion! It has numerous layers, multiple aspects and components, and we'll need to "peel" it to fully reveal its heart. We'll start peeling the concept in the pages that follow, but for now, here's a concise definition:

Hospitality is an <u>attitude</u> of the heart (love) expressed through a <u>lifestyle</u> of giving and serving. It's the giving of your time, talents and resources. It's the giving of yourself!

And to be crystal clear, the practice of hospitality is NOT the same as modern entertaining! Although the two share some of the same components, such as food and socializing, and both are connected to celebrations and holidays, the similarities end there. However, even in their similarities, the two concepts are worlds apart. For instance, as we'll later explain, in modern entertaining food plays a vastly different role than in hospitality. Time for a little clarification?

There are numerous *major* differences between these two very different approaches to social interaction. We can't go into all of them here—we thoroughly explore the subject in a forthcoming book—but we *do* discuss most of them in the chapters that follow.

The main irreconcilable difference is that modern entertaining is a *secular pursuit*, rooted in the social values of an increasingly secularized society. It is a pursuit influenced and often motivated by materialism, competition, and perfectionism. Modern entertaining has no spiritual component, and hence, there is no eternal significance or consequence to the pursuit.

Hospitality, on the other hand, is a *spiritual practice* which is expressed in a practical physical context. It's rooted in Godly values, and prompted by the virtues of love, generosity, humility, and service. (Do you remember our definition?) Hospitality has both physical *and* spiritual components, and hence, it produces results that have both a temporal effect as well as *eternal* significance and consequences. We'll discuss this aspect more, in a later chapter.

Furthermore, hospitality—unlike its secular coun- terpart—is linked to the ministry of angels! During its sacred practice, we reach out and interact with our fel- low man, *not* as though we're mere mortal creatures of flesh and blood, but rather with the awareness that we are *spiritual* beings housed in physical bodies.

We do not simply *entertain* (in the modern sense); instead, understanding that people are comprised of spirit, soul, and body, we minister to the whole individ- ual. In other words, we not only supply a meal, but we also provide nourishment for the soul, enriching the lives of others with love, encouragement, and the truth about our Lord. We literally become God's messengers in practical and beneficial ways—accomplishing the work of the angels!

The Heart of the Matter

So, those who practice hospitality become God's hands extended, His angels on earth. But there's another side to the coin: those who benefit from our hospitality are also "angels"! After all, *everyone* has a spark of the divine within them, and *everyone* has a special story to tell, an experience to relate, a message to share. Once we understand this, we'll begin to see that *angelic* messengers arrive in a variety of shapes, sizes, colors and backgrounds. And ministering to God's "angels" is one of life's true privileges—a privilege which carries with it many surprises and rewards!

Another major difference between Biblical Hospitality and modern entertaining has to do with purpose. Face it, the very word *entertain* means "to amuse or engage in a distraction." In the secular concept of entertaining, people get together to eat, socialize and enjoy special occasions together, such as birthdays, or activities such as watching a televised sporting event. But how well do people really get to know one another while entertaining (or being "entertained")? Usually not very well, because the emphasis is on the food and activities—not the people assembled.

Besides, activities, crowds, and a lot of commotion, typical situations in most social gatherings, don't provide the best atmosphere for people to share their hearts. Which is why entertaining is usually nothing more than a social nicety of no great importance. Strong words, we know, but read on. We'll more than justify our statement.

Please understand there's absolutely nothing wrong with entertaining (social interaction on a superficial level) because, after all, God created us as *social* beings, who enjoy and need relationships. That's why God gave Adam a companion, and also why He created the institution of marriage—the *first* institution He ever created, and one which remains the basis of the family and the foundation of every civilization since the beginning of time.

God said, "It is not good for the man to be alone. I will make a helper suitable for him." (Genesis 2:18 NIV) "...God created mankind in his own image, in the image of God He created them; male and female He created them." (Genesis 1:27 NIV)

Although modern entertaining certainly has its place in our world, and although it can provide pleasant times, simply enjoying a good meal, engaging in light conversation, and playing a game of bridge are NOT life-changing! So what's lacking? The sense of *purpose* that resides in the heart of an angel!

In contrast to modern entertaining, Biblical Hospitality accomplishes all of the above "good times," but its main purpose is establishing, developing, and nurturing relationships—both with God and our fellow travelers in life. Hospitality goes far beyond hanging out with friends and family; it's about tearing down the social walls that divide us, and building bridges between people who otherwise don't "connect"; it's about arranging those "divine connections" where mutual messengers (angels) are able share, and God is able to restore and repair!

We get the word *hospitality* from the Latin *hospitalis*. We also take our idea of "hospital" from this Latin word, which is wholly appropriate: a hospital is a place of healing and restoration, and that's the true focus of hospitality. When we practice Biblical Hospitality, opening up our hearts and homes to others, we become God's conduits of healing and restoration. Through us, God is able to pour on "the oil and wine" for weary and hurting people. (Just as the Good Samaritan did, in Luke 10:34.) We become His hands extended, and our homes become mini-hospitals, an oasis of rest and refreshing in a "parched and dry" world.

Some might say, "*My* house is my *home!* Not a clinic for troubled people!" No less an authority than the Apostle Paul counters with the commandment: "Share each other's burdens, and in this way obey the law of Christ." (Galatians 6:2 NLT) This verse nicely dovetails into Christ's teachings on servanthood and steward-ship, because to accomplish this command, God expects us to use whatever means we have at hand; essentially all the wonderful things He's graciously given us—such as the roofs over our heads! And the bottom line here, is that there's no better avenue for addressing and meeting needs than by practicing hospitality ... in our homes!

John Hagee, Senior Pastor of Cornerstone Church in San Antonio, Texas, once stated, "People are in the middle of a storm. [A test, trial or challenge] Or have just come out of one. Or are going to face one in the future." Hospitality in our homes provides people with a little warmth and shelter in the midst of the storms of life.

Sooner or later, we all go through storms. Having an "angel" on our side helps us to weather them—a hospitable messenger of God's love, hope and ac-ceptance, who opens the door, invites us in, and pro-vides a safe haven; who feeds us with both physical and spiritual food, takes the time to listen, and then lends a helping hand.

The sacred practice of hospitality can provide all the fun and good times of modern entertaining, but unlike its secular counterpart, hospitality is NOT just a "social nicety" of no great importance. Hospitality goes way beyond having a good time, because it serves a higher purpose: there are lives to touch, hearts to mend, needs to meet ... and angels to encounter!

Hospitality is expressing love in a practical way through simple acts of kindness, one person at a time. It can be as significant as the examples we've discussed, but it can also be as simple as a smile, a polite gesture, or a hearty greeting; it can be taking the time to acknowledge an individual with a compliment or an encouraging word; it can even be praying on someone's behalf; and it can take place anywhere and at any time.

Jesus said, "I'm giving you a new commandment ... to love one another. Just as I have loved you, you also should love one another. This is how everyone will know that you are my disciples, if you have love for one another." (John 13:34-35 ISV) The practice of hospitality is how we fulfill this new commandment.

The message of hospitality is: "You are special, and you matter to me *and* God! And you're not alone! I'm here for you, and I welcome you into my life!" Or, as Bobby Schuller frequently states during his weekly *Hour of Power* television ministry, "God loves you—and so do we!" The message of hospitality expresses the heart of an angel!

When we develop the heart of an angel, we can reach the people God strategically sends our way. We can minister to their physical, emotional and spiritual needs, and we can refresh, uplift, and encourage their weary souls. And we usually discover that the people to whom we minister tend to help us in return. They are, after all, angels just like us, each with a unique message of their own. Hence, practicing hospitality is never all give and no take. It's another of God's win-win strategies for abundant living!

We have an expression in life, for people who go out of their way to help us or grant us a favor. We often say it when someone watches the kids (or pets) while we're out of town, runs an errand, or takes us on a shopping trip or to a doctor's appointment.

We say it when someone helps us with a difficult move or an elaborate home repair; or when we're feeling overwhelmed and someone helps us to realize everything's going to work out. And we exclaim it whenever there's a problem, such as a flat tire or an overheated radiator, and someone seems to show up just in the nick of time. With relief and gratitude, we proclaim, "You're an angel!"

When we're loving and helpful, welcoming and accepting, our Lord proudly exclaims, "You're an angel!" It's actually another version of "Well done, good and faithful servant!" (Matthew 25:21 ESV) And when we have the heart of an angel, we'll let people know we're in their corner, we'll call and comfort them, we'll send cards and take meals, we'll ladle on a little tender loving care; and our TLC will bring the world that much closer to God! For the heart of an angel, above all else, is hospitable!

Hospitable people are sensitive and considerate. They find ways to help, and then roll up their sleeves. They tend to bring out the best in us, and make us smile. They add value to our lives, and make our days brighter. We enjoy being around them, and when we visit them in their homes, we don't want to leave! We want to hang out with them all the time, because through them we can sense and experience the love of God!

We need these messengers of God's love more than ever today: "angels" who are willing to open their hearts, their homes, and their lives—through the sacred practice of hospitality. More than ever, people are hurting; they're lonely, often fearful, overwhelmed and stressed out. Many of them have lost faith; all of them need a listening ear and a little TLC.

They need someone who can come along beside them, through good times and bad, and bring comfort; they need someone who's a messenger of love, hope and acceptance, someone who can also point them to the Lord, reminding them that "God has said, 'I will never fail you. I will never abandon you.'" (Hebrews 13:5 NLT)

Friends, these hurting, lonely, fearful, overwhelmed and stressed out people need someone like YOU! Someone with the heart of ... hospitality—who'll leave them better off than the way they met them; who'll make them feel as though they were touched by an angel!

CHAPTER 2:
THE *ART* OF AN ANGEL?

What does hospitality have in common with onions? Glad you asked. Before we can answer, though, we must first discuss the wonders of this pseudo-veggie, which belongs to the same family of plants that includes garlic and chives.

The onion is extremely versatile, and to quote a Spanish idiom (translated, of course), it continually shows up in the soup! Not to mention sauces, stews, and chili; omelets, quiches, and souffles; casseroles, vegetable dishes, and all kinds of sandwiches. But sometimes this ensemble player even takes center stage, in crunchy onion rings or as one of those big beautiful flowering onions that feeds everyone at the table!

George Washington used to chow down on a raw one whenever he felt a cold coming on, because onions are chock full of Vitamin C. We're not sure if doing this warded off the cold, but it sure kept Martha away! And way back in 1648, onions were the first thing the Pilgrims planted in the New World. Europeans brought

19

the versatile veggie with them to North America, but they needn't have bothered: Native Americans already knew all about onions, and used them in cooking, medicinal poultices, and dyes!

Athletes in Ancient Greece ate lots of onions, believing they "balanced" the blood. Roman gladiators were rubbed down with onion juice to firm up their muscles, and in the Middle Ages, people could even pay their rent with onions. Doctors also frequently pre-scribed onions to relieve headaches, coughs, snakebite, and hair loss. And get this, the ancient Egyptians actually worshipped the onion! They believed its spherical shape and concentric rings symbolized eternal life. Whatever.

Onions are a lot like life, love and relationships: they take many differing forms. There are common onions, available in three colors (yellow onions, red onions, white onions). There are wild onions, spring onions, scallions, and pearl onions. Onions come fresh, frozen, dehydrated, and canned. They can be chopped, pickled, caramelized, minced, and even granulated. All this variety, all this utility, reminds us of the diverse-ness of relationships, and the many turns that life can take.

And like an onion, life and people have multiple layers. Our experiences in this world are like periodical-ly peeling back another layer of the "onion" to reveal new mysteries, new opportunities, and new lessons. And the same can be said of relationships: in order to truly get to know someone—and to fully understand why we do the strange, idiosyncratic things that we *all* do—we again need to peel back the layers that insulate people from people.

Onions and Life are fascinating and many splen-dored things! So are onions and people, all of which reminds us of a favorite verse: "How numerous are your works, LORD! You have made them all wisely; the earth is filled with your creations." (Psalm 104:124 ISV)

Without onions, food (and life) would be a little bland! But didn't we promise to compare the onion to hospitality?

Since onions remind us of life, love and relationships, the popular veggie can also represent the Biblical concept of hospitality: God intended the practice of hospitality to be an integral part of LIFE; LOVE is its defining attribute; and RELATIONSHIPS are one of its many benefits! And without hospitality, life would be pretty bland!

But wait, there's more!

Like the onion, hospitality has many layers! At first glance of the outer skin of the concept, one might think it's the same as modern entertaining, just a social nicety of no great importance. But once we begin to peel away the layers (the many facets of hospitality, such as love, service, generosity....) we discover there's more here than meets the eye: fresh layers that reveal a higher purpose than just entertaining; a rich aroma that draws us to greater goals than simply having a good time; and a strong flavor that reminds us of the main mission of hospitality, establishing and nurturing *stronger* relationships with onions. *Uh*, we mean "angels" ... of all kinds!

And yet, we take the concept of hospitality for granted. We think we know all about it, but like the onion, the practice tends to get overlooked. In fact, because very few people go to the trouble of peeling back its layers, hospitality is one of the most neglected and misunderstood concepts in our society today! And when something is misunderstood, inevitably it's also devalued, de-emphasized, and sometimes even disparaged. Hence, it ceases to be an important part of our lives.

Hospitality was once one of our most important endeavors. Not anymore! Just look around when you leave your home: people no longer acknowledge each other on the street; on the job, coworkers are guarded and distant; and even weekly worshippers may sit in a certain section or pew for years, never mingling, never getting to know the folks on the other side of sanctuary! But the numerous signs of inhospitality go on and on.

One reason for our unwelcoming, unsociable, and entirely unfavorable behavior is that fewer and fewer people are reaching out and, specifically, extending invitations to their homes. That's the best place to get to know one another, but we're often too "busy" to bother. Indeed, even within our faith communities, we tend to pack the Sabbath with so many activities we don't have enough time for one of our most important duties, practicing hospitality. According to Gordon Robertson, host of *The 700 Club*, even the once traditional Sunday dinner, where friends, family—and especially newcomers— bonded by breaking bread, is gradually disappearing.

"Sunday dinners are a time to gather together with family and friends to share the events of our lives and enjoy a wonderful home-cooked meal," states Robertson in his web-series *Sunday Dinners: Cooking with Gordon* (at CBN.com). Robertson is a big proponent of restoring the sacred culinary tradition—and so are we!

Jesus Christ commanded His followers to "Love your neighbor as yourself." (Matthew 22:39 NIV) But how can we *love* our neighbor if we don't first take the time to get to *know* our neighbor? Truthfully, we can't— at least, not in the practical and meaningful way our Lord intends! (And by the way, your "neighbors" are not just the couple next door, or the kids down the street;

neighbor encompasses all the "angels" we encounter daily.)

Neglecting to practice hospitality, the main objective of which is to build and strengthen relationships—and thus foster unity—has resulted in "anemic" homes, communities and faith congregations. Our relationships, or the lack there of, are greatly suffering. More and more, people are becoming isolated and *insulated.* They hang out with the family of their favorite sitcom, or "interact" with their cyber-friends on social media. None of which is a suitable substitute for developing *real* friends, the kind that will be there for you in both good times and bad.

There is, after all, tremendous wisdom in Proverbs 18:24, "One who has unreliable friends soon comes to ruin, but there is a friend who sticks closer than a brother." (NIV)

Nevertheless, we continue to neglect God's sacred practice. And to add insult to injury, even the word *hospitality* is slowly fading from our social vocabulary. Frequent comments consist of variations of: "I love to entertain"; "They have the perfect house for entertaining"; or "She has a flair for entertaining"!

In TV shows such as HGTV's *Property Brothers* and *House Hunters*, we hear prospective homeowners say things like "We need a big house with a gourmet kitchen, so we can entertain." Once these reality show participants finally purchase the house, or remodel it, we hear them exclaim "Now we'll be able to entertain!"

Why not say, "Now we can extend hospitality"? Actually, in such cases, we'd rather they didn't! Because what these people have in mind is NOT the Biblical concept initiated by God. And, when "hospitality" *is* used, it's generally in relation to the hospitality industry (hotels and restaurants), which is a sad use of the word.

If you think about it, "hospitality industry" is an oxymoron. How can a business ever hope to manufacture and sell love, hope, and acceptance? How can a company be about the "business" of the angels? Hospitality is about building relationships, not making money! Even the Beatles understood this one, when they sang "money can't buy me love."

We don't know about you, but right about now we could really go for a nice crisp onion—*No, wait!*—we mean some *genuine* hospitality!

In the pages that follow, we'll peel back the onion of hospitality to further strip away the misconceptions clinging to it. We'll examine each intricate layer of the sacred practice, revealing its wonders, until we reach the delectable core of the concept, the *truth!* During the process of preparing our "onion," we may bring a tear or two, or make you hungry for some genuine hospitality; but when we're finished, we hope and believe you'll have a better (Biblical) understanding of hospitality and its importance in God's plan for life.

Cutting to the Truth!

The first misconception about hospitality that we'll strip away, is that it's the same thing as modern entertaining. As we stated in Chapter 1, the practice of God's sacred command often shares the same elements with its secular counterpart, such as fun, food, social activities and celebrations, but the similarities between the two *end* there. Hospitality is NOT the same as modern entertaining! Unfortunately, this association continues to confuse the issue and further fuels this *major* misconception of the divine practice.

This one overriding misconception has led to every other erroneous idea about hospitality. Confusing God's Biblical concept with modern entertaining has only led to more misunderstandings, and has created the stumbling block that results in people neglecting the practice of hospitality. It's time to cut the ties that bind us to a secular conceit, and blind us to the truth.

As we previously stated, there are two major differences between these two approaches to social interaction:

Modern entertaining is a secular pursuit with no spiritual component or eternal consequences; and hence, no angels! Hospitality is a spiritual practice with BOTH physical and spiritual components, BOTH temporal and eternal consequences; and hence, it makes room for "angels" of all types (the wide variety of human *messengers* who have a story to tell, an experience to relate, a message to share; and for all followers of the God of the Bible, the main message should be LOVE).

Modern entertaining provides a pleasant occasion with no purpose greater than eating and having a good time; and as such, it is no more than a social nicety of no great importance. Hospitality can provide food and good times, but it serves a *higher* purpose: meeting needs, healing hearts, touching lives, and even encountering angels! Because there are higher stakes involved, and eternal consequences that go beyond having fun, hospitality is NOT just a social nicety that can be neglected if and when we choose.

Let's peel back a little more of the hospitality onion to reveal another big difference between these two vastly different approaches to social activity:

> Today, the pursuit of <u>modern entertaining</u> is considered an art. An "art" requires a set of skills and creative ability; and only after years of pursuit, can the artist truly "master" it. Indeed, the art of entertainment requires that one have culinary, creative, organizational, and social skills, as well as a bit of sophistication and an extensive knowledge of proper etiquette. Because there are certain standards the entertaining host must strive to meet, properly executing the art requires a great deal of time, effort and money.
>
> Additionally, the art must be executed in the proper setting. Do you remember those people on the HGTV reality show, who exclaimed—only after buying a new home or remodeling an old kitchen— "*Now* we can entertain"? The art of entertaining is responsible for making people think they need big houses with hardwood floors, the finest furnishings, and custom window treatments; or elaborate designer kitchens filled with granite countertops and state-of-the-art appliances; or formal dining rooms loaded with fine china, glistening silver, and heirloom linens. The motto of the art of entertaining is "Nothing but the best to impress!"

When you're entertaining, preparing and serving a gourmet meal is an absolute must. Each and every dish must be a culinary masterpiece, and regardless of who cooked (or catered) the meal, everyone must be told that all the food was prepared from scratch using only the finest ingredients ... many of which were either raised in the backyard garden or freshly slaughtered from the livestock grazing on the south 40. *Moo!*

Yes, we're exaggerating, but things can really get a bit elaborate in the art of entertainment. Think "Martha Stewart" and any of a number of her televised holiday specials, where the tablescape is enough to impress the crowned heads of Merry Old England; where the lawn is immaculately manicured, the house newly painted and absolutely spotless; where everything from the food to the music to the family dog (just back from the groomers and on her best behavior) are picture P-E-R-F-E-C-T! *Ooh la la!*

Isn't this what comes to mind when you think of entertaining? If so, you're thinking is on the right track, because entertaining is, after all, an art!

Okay, it's time for the practice of hospitality to weigh in. But we're tired of typing, so we'll sum things up by stating:

Hospitality is a matter of the heart, *not* the art!

Unlike modern entertaining, the sacred practice of hospitality is NOT an art, it's a Biblical command. It doesn't get caught up in a lot of *foofoo!* Such trappings can be nice, but they aren't necessary. What is required is your LOVE! And furthermore, when the Apostle Peter said, "Cheerfully share your home with those who need a meal or a place to stay," (1 Peter 4:9 NLT) he didn't qualify his command by saying, "Uh, that is, *if* you have a gorgeous home with a designer kitchen!"

In a more straight-forward translation of this verse, the Apostle puts it this way: "Be hospitable to one another without complaint." (1 Peter 4:9 NASB) The word **be** pretty much rules out having a choice in the matter. He doesn't say "try to be"; it's a command! Period. Done deal. We don't even get to complain about it. The Apostle doesn't give us room for any BUTs. He doesn't command us to be hospitable only *if* we're outgoing "people-persons," or *if* we're gourmet cooks, or *if* we have lots of free time and extra money, or *if* we're highly sophisticated and have our etiquette down pat, or *if* we've mastered the art of entertainment.

Trust us, the Big Fisherman didn't care about any of that stuff. He just wanted us to reach out to our neighbors in genuine hospitality. And while we're on the subject, when this brawny giant of a man, whose hands were thickly calloused from hauling in his fishing nets, commanded us to be hospitable, he was NOT address-ing just the womenfolk. Guys, he was also talking 'bout you!

Hey, ladies, stop laughing! Allow us to point out that there *were* women present when the Apostle issued his historic command, and again, Peter never said, Be hospitable—*if* you're the Martha Stewart-type who's mastered the art of entertaining!

Now's the perfect time to list several aspects of the practice of hospitality (layers of the "onion")—which are absent in the art of entertaining. Hospitality is:

- *a sacred commandment to be obeyed by both men and women*
- *a key qualification for spiritual leadership (both in our churches and in our homes)*
- *a defining characteristic of a Godly man or woman*
- *a practical means of expressing God's love*
- *an effective approach to loving one's "neighbor"*

- *an occasion to make room for "the stranger"*
- *an appointment to encounter angels (any heaven-sent messengers)*
- *a standard practice of reaching out to the poor and needy (the "least" among us)*
- *an instrument for meeting needs and alleviating suffering*
- *an avenue for encouraging and refreshing people*
- *a method of sharing the Good News of Jesus Christ*
- *an antidote for selfishness and isolation*
- *a tool to break down walls and build bridges*
- *a stimulus for true fellowship (or koinónia)*
- *a forum for connecting and building genuine relationships*
- *a catalyst for unifying the family and the Body of Christ*
- *an opportunity to make a positive contribution in the lives of others*
- *a springboard to fun and social interaction*
- *a path to Christian maturity*
- *a way to leave a legacy!*

We'll discuss all of these "layers" in subsequent chapters. For now, however, it should be clear that regardless of our gender, and regardless of whether or not we've mastered the art of entertaining, we're still called to practice hospitality. But to restate the matter, we don't have to be adept in the art, because the Biblical concept of <u>hospitality is NOT a matter of the art; it's a matter of the heart</u>.

It's not about gourmet food and designer homes; instead of focusing on such external matters, the sacred practice focuses on the matters of the heart (love, hope, healing). It's not about "perfection" (obsessing over every little detail); it's about relationships.

We'll continue to peel the onion of hospitality in the chapters that follow, further revealing the *heart*—NOT the *art* of an angel.

CHAPTER 3:
YOU, TOO,
CAN BE AN ANGEL!

Jesus said, "If you love me, obey my commandments."
For "Those who accept my commandments and obey
them are the ones who love me." (John 14:15 and 21
NLT) This is a heavy-duty truth. Clearly, with no ifs,
ands, or buts about it, Christ fully expects everyone
who follows Him to "carry out His orders"—including
the command to "be hospitable"!

But our Lord would never ask us to do something
we weren't capable of; a task for which we were ill-
equipped. God knows exactly what we need to get the
job done....

As we stated in the last chapter, hospitality is NOT
an art. An art requires special skills and abilities. If you
happen to already have such talents, then *excellent!* You
can put them to good use when practicing hospitality.
They will certainly enhance your efforts, but they are
not required, because there are no high, artistic
standards to be met in hospitality. The food and

surroundings don't have to be picture-perfect. All that *is* required is LOVE.

Let's review the definition of hospitality:

Hospitality is an <u>attitude</u> of the heart (love) expressed through a <u>lifestyle</u> of giving and serving. It's the giving of your time, talents and resources (but ONLY whatever those may be). It's the giving of yourself! (There are no rules etched in stone.)

Practicing hospitality is about expressing love in a practical way. *How* you express that love is totally up to you, NOT the demands and dictates of the art of entertaining. Your own unique methods will depend on your personality, time and resources, and your basic approach to life and socializing, which is generally determined by your upbringing or background.

We're all different! Each of us has our own individual style. In hospitality, there is no "one size fits all" approach to social interaction or planning a gathering. For instance, some people are by nature more formal or traditional, while others may be more casual or laid-back. Some people enjoy being more lavish, others more simplistic in their approach to hosting guests. It's all good!

The Apostle Peter reassures us, "Each of you should use whatever gift you have received to serve others, as faithful stewards of God's grace in its various forms." (1 Peter 4:10 NIV) Peter is acknowledging that we all have something to contribute, we all have our own special talents and style; but *whatever* we have, we're expected to use it to minister to others. He's saying, "You, too, can be an angel"!

If you don't have the culinary skills to prepare a gourmet dinner, but you *can* cook a simple meal that's nourishing and served with love, then you can be an angel of hospitality. If on the other hand, you simply don't have the time or energy to prepare a meal, you can still get together with someone and share a pizza or Chinese take-out. We've actually gotten to know people really well over nothing more than a cup of coffee and a few cookies. If you believe that you can, too, and if you're willing to start reaching out, then you're on your way to being an angel.

Extending hospitality doesn't require a lot of time, effort or money. God is mainly concerned that we connect with people and give of ourselves. In practicing hospitality, He wants us to share our time, talents, and resources, but He doesn't expect us to give what we don't have, or can't afford. Even if we have only enough time to talk to someone on the phone, or send them a card (or a text or an e-mail), letting them know that we care and are thinking of them, we're *still* doing the work of the angels.

If we meet at a restaurant or a coffee shop, or pack a couple of sandwiches and bond on a bench in the park while feeding the squirrels, we're still doing the work of the angels. As long as we're reaching out to people, to develop and nurture relationships, we can be like the angels! The key is to be sensitive to the needs of others and use our opportunities to touch lives. That's called being hospitable.

Which brings us to another big difference between modern entertaining and Biblical Hospitality:

The practice of hospitality is a simpler, less demanding, less time-consuming, and less expensive way to socialize than its secular counterpart. It's also far less stressful, because unlike modern entertaining, it's not your food, house, or artistic skills that are on display; what is on display is your heart, demonstrated through your love.

As for creating the "proper setting," in hospitality a big designer home "perfect for entertaining" is not required. If you happen to have one, that's great! Because you can share it with others! But if you're like most of us, and your house is comfortable but a little less extravagant—be it ever so humble—your home is still the perfect place to extend hospitality.

Picture the house of a beloved grandmother: perhaps her home is nothing to particularly brag about, but there's always something else inside that's truly inviting. What is it? The gourmet cuisine, the Better-Homes-and-Gardens interior decorating? We visited Grandma one day, and this is what *we* discovered: her home was small. The rooms were distinguished by old furnishings and outdated decor.

Whenever we visited her, and we did so frequently, we always ended up in her kitchen; it's where she overfed us, and where we sat for hours, stuffed, happy, and chatting across the table. Grandma's table was set with mix-matched dishes, paper napkins, and oddly-placed silverware, all atop a tablecloth that really didn't go with anything. Her meals were simple fare, basically the Southern foods Tom had grown up with, but ... *Ooh!* How delicious! Being a Northerner, Wilma was thrilled by the awesome taste and crispiness of her fried pork chops. "It's just her usual hearty fare," Tom would say nonchalantly. "She breads the chops with crushed, seasoned, cornflakes."

Her "usual fare," the meal she had prepared with no fuss and no pretension, tasted absolutely gourmet. It was simply divine! When Wilma asked her where she got the recipe, Grandma simply shrugged and said she couldn't rightly remember: "I was just using whatever I had in the cupboard." Now, obviously there was a little something extra in that cupboard. In fact, something filled her entire humble home, which made it lovely and welcoming. Can you guess what it was?

Whatever Grandma lacked in decor, what she never even cared to know about "style"; she made up for—with something far more precious: her love! You see, Grandma understood what it takes to be an angel: it's all about *attitude!*

The Attitude of an Angel

There's a lot of truth to the old adage, "It's not as important WHAT you say, as HOW you say it!" Similarly, how and why we do something is just as important as the act. That's why the Apostle Peter warns us, "Show hospitality to one another without grumbling." (1 Peter 4:9 ESV) To properly obey God's commandment to be hospitable, we first need to have the right attitude. If you'll recall our definition, hospitality is an *attitude* of the heart (LOVE)!

Attitude affects everything we think and do, and God wants us to have the right attitude—especially when ministering to others! For instance, we should never extend hospitality out of a sense of obligation. Love must always be the impetus for any act of kindness.

When asked, what is the greatest commandment? Jesus replied, "'Love the Lord your God with all your heart and with all your soul and with all your mind.' This is the first and greatest commandment. And the second is like it: 'Love your neighbor as yourself.' All the

Law and the Prophets hang on these two command-ments." (Matthew 22:36-40 NIV; see also Leviticus 19:18)

We can fulfill both these commandments when we ungrudgingly practice hospitality with a loving, caring, positive attitude: we'll be loving *God* by keeping His commandments; and we'll be loving our "neighbor" with genuine acts of kindness.

Interestingly, right before the Apostle Peter admon-ishes us to be hospitable, he states "...Above all things have fervent love among yourselves: for love shall cover a multitude of sins." (1 Peter 4:8 King James 2000) By *fervent* love, the apostle means for us to love intensely, zealously, and earnestly. In other words, God wants us to be *active* and *diligent* in our love for others.

Fervent love is also the kind of love that perseveres. Even in those times when we don't feel like it! And why not? After all, "to love" is a decision we make, not an emotion. It's an act of the will, not just a warm fuzzy feeling. Although feelings and emotions generally ac-company love, we can't always count on them to moti-vate us to do the right thing. In fact, if we start relying on the way we *feel*, many of us may decide to just go back to bed and hide under the covers. That's *not* the attitude of an angel. God's messengers (that would be us) understand that love is a commitment.

And it's a fervent, commitment to love that "covers a multitude of sins,"—from minor aggravations to major slights—enabling us to make *allowances* for people when they're not at their best, instead of *excuses* for not interacting with them. Fervent love helps us to overlook their faults, to give them the benefit of the doubt, and to cut people a little slack.

Hey, we can all use a little slack when we're being pulled in different directions, our patience is stretched thin, and are nerves are taut. That's why Jesus said,

"God blesses those who are merciful, for they will be shown mercy." (Matthew 5:7 NLT)

Maintaining an attitude of fervent love means we'll be committed to quickly forgive an offense, big or small, as well as the offender. We won't retaliate, and we won't hold a grudge. Instead, we'll choose to take the high road; and when the emotional wound hurts, we'll present it to God in prayer, asking Him to heal the hurt. No, it's *not* an easy path to tread, but it's *always* for the best: "Work at living in peace with everyone.... Look after each other so that none of you fails to receive the grace of God. Watch out that no poisonous root of bitterness grows up to trouble you, corrupting many." (Hebrews 12:14-15 NLT) If you do this, you'll be walking with the angels!

We are all flawed creatures. Sooner or later, whether intentionally or not, we're going do *something* that's going to hurt *someone*. At times, we'll be insensitive or selfish or even a little nasty to someone. It's our *natural* inclination. But adopting an attitude of fervent love, making a commitment to respond in a Godly way (instead of *re-acting* naturally) reveals the hospitable heart of an angel. It's a character trait God wants us to develop, because God is all about love. It helps us overlook the faults in others, and it covers our own shortcomings, as well.

In the Bible's quintessential chapter on the subject, the Apostle Paul characterizes Godly love. He writes, "Love is patient, love is kind. It does not envy, it does not boast, it is not proud. It does not dishonor others, it is not self-seeking, it is not easily angered, it keeps no record of wrongs. Love does not delight in evil but rejoices with the truth. It always protects, always trusts, always hopes, always perseveres. Love never fails." (1 Corinthians 13:4-8 NIV)

The practice of hospitality begins and ends with this kind of love; it's the foundation, the motivation, and the modus operandi for touching lives and building relationships through the sacred practice. It's the only true requirement of hospitality, the only real standard— because unlike modern entertaining, it's *not* an art.

Love is *the* attitude of an angel, but in regards to hospitality, the "right" attitude is also shaped by one's PERSPECTIVE. Not surprisingly, this truth points to yet another big difference between modern entertaining and God's original concept: people who entertain may view the secular pursuit from a number of varying perspectives; but those who practice hospitality should share a single *Heavenly* perspective.

Honestly, in order to be *willing* to fully obey the Biblical command to be hospitable, and to really appreciate the tremendous value of the sacred practice in God's eternal economy, one absolutely *must* be able to see people and possessions from God's point of view. In other words, one must gain, and view life from, a Heavenly perspective.

The Hospitable God of the Bible created each of us in His own image. When He views us, He sees our great potential for good, and He highly values every single one of us! In fact, He cherishes us so much that He gave up His only Son in order to save us! (John 3:16) In God's eyes, we're all worth the trouble of going the extra mile! (Matthew 5:41)

Case in point: Jesus stated,

I was hungry, and you fed me. I was thirsty, and you gave me a drink. I was a stranger, and you invited me into your home. I was naked, and you gave me clothing. I was sick, and you cared for me. I was in prison, and you visited me.

Then [the righteous] will reply, "Lord, when did we ever see you hungry and feed you? Or thirsty and give you something to drink? Or a stranger and show you hospitality? Or naked and give you clothing? When did we ever see you sick or in prison and visit you?" (Matthew 25:35-39 NLT)

The Lord's reply? "In solemn truth I tell you that in so far as you rendered such services to one of the humblest of these My brethren, you rendered them to Myself." (Matthew 25:40 Weymouth NT) The King James Version words it this way: "Inasmuch as ye have done *it* unto one of the least of these My brethren, ye have done *it* unto Me."

God clearly (and *literally*) takes our acts of kindness *personally!* So when we meet a need or just do something nice for someone, we actually touch the heart of God! Once we realize this, we'll understand that, at least on a spiritual level, we're not actually serving and giving to those around us. Of course, we *are*, in the natural sense—and they definitely reap the benefits—but the ultimate recipient is our Lord!

This sobering truth is called the Unto Him Principle, and it means that any and all of the preparations you make for your guests, and whatever you do to make people feel welcome and special, is really done for the Lord! Any expression of love, any act of hospitality, any smile, any little prayer or thoughtful courtesy or word of encouragement ... it should all be done as though God is the true recipient (And He is!) And these acts of kindness will bring a smile of gratitude to His face!

When we practice hospitality, no matter how many places we set at the table, the guest of honor is always God. Actually, in a manner of speaking, we have only one guest—one great, ultimate, divine guest whom we're serving, honoring, and caring for: the Lord! When we embrace this truth, we'll realize no matter what we do or accomplish in this life, we're really just "playing" to an audience of One! "Therefore whether you eat or drink or whatever you do, do all things to the glory of God." (1 Corinthians 10:31 Berean Literal)

HEAVENLY PERSPECTIVE, LOVE and....

Truth! Lastly, our attitude toward hospitality should be INFORMED: Hospitality is an inescapable Biblical mandate for all of God's people. And, it's a neglected practice that's needed today more than ever.

Don't try to rationalize that hospitality is a command that doesn't apply to you. If you're a follower of Christ, the God of Abraham, Isaac and Israel, you are called to "be hospitable" in both relational *and* practical ways. If you're one of the countless people who routinely tell themselves, *I'd practice hospitality, BUT ... I just don't have the time, or the money, or the right house, or the proper skills....;* or, *I'd practice hospitality, BUT ... I'm a guy, or I'm a woman but it's just not my thing!*—then we implore you, would you PLEASE cut it out! Stop making <u>excuses</u>, and stop finding <u>ways to avoid</u> the sacred practice.

God's family should be the most hospitable people on the planet, known for their love through reaching out, welcoming, accepting, helping, serving, touching lives and building the kinds of meaningful relationships that strengthen our families and bring unity to our communities and places of work and worship. Therefore, we absolutely *must* become God's hands extended, His divine messengers of hospitality! Join us in this fabulous and *indispensable* endeavor, and then ... you, too, can be an angel!

CHAPTER 4:
AN ANGEL NAMED MARTHA

In the early 1980s, at the height of the modern feminist movement, when women were walking out on their husbands to "find themselves"—and leaving behind a sink full of dirty dishes in protest—along came Martha Stewart.

At a time when millions of women were feeling trapped and unfulfilled in their traditional roles—suffering from the "doll's house syndrome" (coined from the Ibsen play)—and were trading in an apron for a briefcase, Martha came with the message that being domestic was not oppressive nor demeaning, but chic and glamorous. Bravo, Martha!

Thanks to Martha, *domestic* was no longer a dirty word. In fact, aided by some remarkable marketing strategies, she indoctrinated women (and some men) into believing that executing a successful social event or running a home efficiently and with great style, took just as much skill and savvy as running a large corporation.

Martha's first book, *Entertaining*, published in 1982,

sold millions of copies, and launched a career that has spanned over three decades, and included a regular television show as well as holiday specials; books, magazines, DVDs, and hundreds of products. That first book certainly paid off for her, but frankly, she's earned every bit of it. She's spent years training with great chefs and perfecting her craft. For instance, in various segments of her show, she's explained how she trained under a Master Sushi Chef, spent hours learning new things in the areas of entertaining and, in general, practiced, practiced, and then practiced some more.

As with any pursuit, practice makes <u>perfect</u>. No one becomes a good cook over night, or learns interior decorating in a weekend. Martha Stewart certainly has paid her dues, and in the process, she's become an American icon who's greatly influenced the way people entertain today. In fact, just mention the word *entertaining* and most people immediately think of her, along with visions of richly appointed rooms, fine dining, and decadent desserts flavored with sugar and spice and everything nice. Actually, not *just* "nice," but PERFECT.

For most people, Martha Stewart is, after all, the embodiment of the <u>perfect</u> host or hostess; someone who possesses culinary, artistic, organizational and social skills; who has all the social graces and an extensive knowledge of etiquette, to know exactly where to position every piece of silverware, what type of glasses to use, which (and how many) courses to serve, and in what order—all the tiny details necessary to pull off a <u>perfect</u> social event. And, of course, she also has the "<u>perfect</u> house(s) for entertaining."

Ms. Stewart is indeed the <u>perfect</u> (Oops, there's that word again!) role model for the art of entertaining. She's the standard bearer, the one countless people aspire to be like, and the one they endlessly try to imitate.

There are, in fact, many "experts" in the field of entertaining, today, but all of them were first inspired by Martha Stewart, and are following the trail she blazed.

A recent trend among both celebrities, as well as everyday folks, is to hire an "event planner" to arrange elaborate social functions—and not just for weddings, which have increasingly become lavish affairs, but also for other occasions. People today even go so far as to hire party planners to coordinate their children's birthday parties, so that there will be clowns, magicians, and other elaborate entertainments. Which seems a bit much, especially when Johnny and Janie are only four! But, hey, mom and dad just want everything to be perfect! (Sigh, we need to check a thesaurus for a word other than....)

The P-word continues to pop up here, which only serves to underscore the point we're making: Martha Stewart is the Angel (or messenger) of Entertaining, but the message she's sending is like a double-edged sword —because modern entertaining cuts two ways.

First, the often elaborate "fixings" of entertaining can be quite enjoyable, and besides, a little elegance and sophistication never hurt anyone! We totally agree on both of these points. It can be fun to throw a fancy party, or dress up for a special occasion. Such celebrations break the monotony of an everyday routine, and can add spice to life. But there's another edge to the secular pursuit, one that can cut like a knife....

If you're going to engage in the art of entertaining, you'll eventually have to meet its sky-high expectations. Everything you do, everything you use, will be weighed against Martha's gold standard of PERFECTION, which means your preparations must be perfect: the food, the drinks, the table settings, the house, the music, every last minor detail. Few people can properly wield the art of entertaining, or handle its heavy expectations—and those who try are frequently wounded by their experiences!

Again, the motto of the art is "Nothing but the best for the guests!" Or, in other words, *Make Martha proud!* In fact, the ultimate compliment for a host or hostess who is "entertaining" sounds like this: "Wow, I'm really impressed! Everything was *perfect.* You're a regular Martha Stewart!" If you're caught up in the art of entertaining, and you receive such compliments, you know you've arrived.

The ultimate aim in the art of entertaining is to pull off a "perfect" social event in which everything goes smoothly and just as planned, with no glitches, no mishaps, no delays; and for which all the preparations are flawless and awe-inspiring. Now, ask yourself, when has anything in life ever been perfect? To paraphrase the great poet Robert Burns, the best-laid plans of mice and men often go awry, and leave us not but pain and grief for promised joy! No, we're NOT pessimistic, but we *are* realistic.

Things *do* come up, and stuff happens, all the time. Even for those masters of entertaining who *are* capable of pulling off a perfect event, there will always be certain circumstances beyond their control and usually unforeseeable: the joy of a "perfect" cookout can be dampened by a sudden cloudburst; and the promise of a juicy cut of meat will eventually dry up if the guests are late and the roast has to tarry too long in an oven set for "warm."

Face it, life is *not* like *Jurassic Park*, for which the motto is "Nothing can go wrong."

On second thought, life is *exactly* like *Jurassic Park*: whatever *can* go wrong, probably *will* go wrong—except in life, people don't end up as lunch for a pack of starving dinosaurs. We make mistakes and suffer failures all the time but, hey, it's okay—Life, and the Creator of Life, are very forgiving. Wish we could say the same thing about the art of entertaining. Can you imagine Martha Stewart, the supreme master of the art, committing a social *faux pas*? Her fresh flower arrangement wilting, her tea being tepid, or her soufflé collapsing? Of course not! When it comes to the art of entertaining, anything less than **PERFECTION** is an unpardonable sin!

In sharp contrast to the art, when practicing Biblical Hospitality, there is no unpardonable sin. That's because there are no lofty standards we're pressured to adhere to, no pretentious protocols enforced by the entertaining "police." No one need worry about their cooking skills, or lack thereof, the kind of home they live in, and whether or not they fussed enough. And everyone measures up! Not only is it all good, but everyone is welcome to participate in the sacred practice, also—including the kids and the family pets. No one gets left out in hospitality!

"Perfect" Little Angels

The ultimate goal of the sacred practice is not to try to look perfect, and not to try to pull off a flawless event; instead, it's all about relationships. *It's not an art, it's a matter of the heart.* And in practicing hospitality, success is measured not by whether the food, the house, and all the other preparations were perfect; but by whether the lines of communication were opened, friendships were formed, people shared their burdens or dreams, laughed or cried together. When the "angels" gathered to relate the messages of their lives, were hearts touched, and emotions healed? If so, the occasion is considered a triumph in the eyes of God!

Please don't misunderstand, we're all for perfection—in the right areas. PERFECTION expresses the nature of God. He is perfect (Psalm 18:30), and in the beginning, He created a perfect world. (Genesis 1:31) Sadly, we had to go and mess things up, by choosing to disobey the first and only commandment God imposed at the time. But the Lord created each of us in His own perfect image, and hence, God intends each of us to be perfect! Perfection is God's ideal, and His ultimate purpose for our lives is that each of us become *perfect* in Him.

Jesus stated, "You therefore must be perfect, as your Heavenly Father is perfect." (Matthew 5:48 ESV) But in this context, the idea of perfection equates to maturity in Christ, or becoming more Godly, something every believer aspires to throughout their existence on this mortal coil, but never fully attains—until they go "home" to spend the rest of eternity with their loving Heavenly Father. Maturing to this state of godly perfection should be the goal of every believer, the target to which we constantly aim.

We're fooling ourselves, however, if we think it's an easy endeavor, or that we won't continually make mistakes or, in some cases, even have to start again at square one. And for those who believe they're already there, all we can write is "LOL!"

The Apostle Paul states, "...Everyone has sinned; we all fall short of God's glorious standard." (Romans 3:23 NLT) But our Heavenly Father understands this, and has made the ultimate allowance for our human frailties: "God, with undeserved kindness, declares that we are righteous [or "perfect" in Christ]. He did this through Christ Jesus when he freed us from the penalty for our sins." (Romans 3:24 NLT)

People often say it's hard to live the Christian life, but that's not true. As Dr. David Jeremiah has stated on his television series *Turning Point*, "It is <u>impossible</u> to live the Christian life! It's only by God's grace." *Grace* is the unearned and unmerited favor of God expressed through His supernatural power and strength. In other words, *we're* not perfect—but our God is! And He helps us to do the best we can in all things at all times.

We often jokingly tell people that the two of us are perfectionists. Like Martha Stewart, we, too, have high standards. But unlike Martha, we're not concerned about the art of entertaining and producing flawless efforts. First of all, we know that's an impossibility. (As we discussed over the last few paragraphs.) Secondly, our "perfectionism" has more to do with pleasing God. We always try to *do* our best and *be* our best, which is His *perfect* will for our lives—because God has called each of us to pursue *excellence.*

The Apostle Paul stated in his letter to the followers of Christ at Philippi, "...This is my prayer: that your love may abound more and more in knowledge and profound insight, so that you may be able to discern what is <u>excellent</u>, and may be pure and blameless for the day of Christ, filled with the fruit of righteousness that comes through Jesus Christ...." (Philippians 1:9-10 Berean SB)

And a few verses later, he admonished them to pursue excellence: "...Whatever is true, whatever is honorable, whatever is just, whatever is pure, whatever is lovely, whatever is commendable, if there is any <u>excellence</u>, if there is anything worthy of praise, think about these things." (Philippians 4:8 ESV)

Be perfect and pursue excellence, *but* avoid the heavy burden of becoming a perfectionist. Confusing? Since words often have different levels of meaning, let's explore God's concept of *perfection* (the pursuit of excellence) versus the world's idea of *perfectionism*. Dr. Monica A. Frank, Ph.D. offers an excellent definition of *perfectionism*: an "individual's belief that he or she must be perfect to be acceptable." Contained within this belief is the conviction that, in order to make the grade, a person's efforts also must be perfect—and this view has never been more true than in the art of entertaining. Dr. Frank continues:

> *Perfectionism is black and white with no gray area. Anything other than perfect is failure. Perfectionism is an attitude, not necessarily a behavior. In other words, two people can engage in the same behavior such as trying to win an Olympic gold medal but one can be pursuing excellence and the other is demanding perfection. The difference lies in the thought process about the goal or behavior, not in the goal or behavior itself.* (ExcelatLife.com)

In this sense of the word, *perfectionism* is the complete opposite of God's ideal for every believer. Regardless of *who* we are or *what* we do, "To the praise of the glory of his grace ... He has made us accepted in the beloved." (Ephesians 1:6 King James 2000) The pursuit of excellence, on the other hand, is the desire to achieve what is excellent, but without all the emotional baggage attached to the "need to be perfect"; or, to quote Dr. Frank, excellence "does not demand a sacrifice of self-esteem, as it tends to focus on the <u>process</u> of achievement rather than the <u>outcome</u>."

In a nutshell, perfectionism is about performing flawlessly and being nothing short of perfect (despite all our flaws and imperfections) with the motive of measuring up. But God's pursuit of excellence focuses on putting your best foot forward and always trying to do the right thing—with the motive of pleasing God and no fear of failure. And guess what? These differences can also be used to contrast the art of entertaining and Biblical Hospitality!

When practicing hospitality, our motives are to please God (by obeying His command to love and serve others); we put our best foot forward, by reaching out and being welcoming; and we try to do the right thing, by treating others the way we ourselves would like to be treated (—applying "The Golden Rule" of Matthew 7:12).

All of this means, there will be times when we really fuss over our guests, God's precious "angels," in an attempt to offer them the best, to make them feel special, and to communicate the truth that God loves them and so do we. But we accomplish this in whatever ways we choose. In hospitality, there are no preset standards we need meet, and hence no fear of failure. In God's divine practice, we always measure up—because, after all, we're doing the work of the angels!

The art of entertaining, however, is all about pulling off the impossible, an absolutely perfect event; about flawlessly *performing* as a true master (or would-be master) of the art; about meeting the lofty standards set by the experts in magazines and on TV (with little regard of your time, true talents, and resources)—with the motive of being *accepted* as ... well, a "regular Martha Stewart." That's a lot of pressure, because by its very nature, pursuing the art can actually open the door to failure and disappointment.

Once more, life is not perfect and neither are we! This is an incontrovertible FACT! Here's another: God expects us to be hospitable. Period. But like life, when reaching out to others, the timing will never be *perfect*; our houses will never be *perfect*; our talents and resources may *seem* less than adequate, and circumstances will always try to get in the way of doing God's will. And few of us will ever live up to the lofty standards of the art of entertaining. So, what can you do?

A More Excellent Way

God has not called us to entertain. He's called us to love. God does not expect us to meet the standards of an art. He expects us to be hospitable. God doesn't want us to use what we don't possess, or perhaps never will. He wants us to give of ourselves, and never more than whatever time, talents and resources we *do* have, and in whichever way we feel best meets people's needs.

God doesn't need us to wow Him with over-the-top *tablescapes* and fancy finger-foods; but He does need us to connect with others, to build and nurture relationships, to be His hands extended. God isn't watching us to see if we can perform like a regular Martha Stewart. But He *is* longing to say, as we extend hospitality, "Well done, good and faithful servant." (Matthew 25:21 NIV)

God doesn't make unreasonable demands with regards to His sacred practice; that's the job of modern entertaining, with its preoccupation with the high standards of an art. Unlike all the high-profile entertaining gurus, with their endless flow of well-meaning, albeit overwhelming advice and daunting demands, God never places such a heavy load upon our backs. In fact, with respect to the practice of hospitality—which is directed by love, not dictated by the art of entertaining—we can easily apply the Lord's reminder that, "...My yoke is easy to bear, and the burden I give you is light." (Matthew 11:30 NLT)

Practicing hospitality has never required perfection. But sadly, because most people have confused the

Biblical concept with modern entertaining, they imagine God's sacred command to have all sorts of strings attached, all of which are ready to entangle the unwary. Nothing is further from the truth. These uninformed people *do*, however, bring numerous complications to the practice. They tie it up with the art, and strangle it in issues of perfection. As we've stated, they erroneously believe all their efforts must be perfect; they also believe their surroundings have to be perfect—as well as the timing.

The only earthly things actually tied to hospitality are LIFE: imperfect, ill-timed, ill-opportune, ill-equipped life; simple, satisfying, beautiful life, perfectly conceived by the Creator of the Universe; and PEOPLE: flawed and fallible, fearfully and wonderfully made; both of which happily and blessedly remain imperfect! Hence, there will never be a *perfect* time to extend hospitality. You'll never have everything just right, or feel just fine.

In fact, if you wait for the *perfect* opportunity—after you've had your grass manicured by the lawn doctor; or your home's undergone complete remodeling by the "Property Brothers"; or you've installed a designer kitchen with the "Kitchen Cousins"; or you've replaced your everyday stuff with the best China, crystal and linens money can buy; or you've gotten around to hiring an expert in interior decor such as Candace Olson—you'll never get around to it. But if you do, after achieving all the above, you'll probably also be ready for a long vacation in Bedlam!

If you're going to wait till your pooch has been trained by the "Dog Whistler"; or your kids return from finishing school; or your spouse loses weight, gets plastic surgery, and starts looking like Chris Hemsworth or Sofia Vergara ... then forget it! *It ain't gonna happen!*

Sure, we're having a little fun in order to make a point: if you wait for the so-called perfect time and circumstances, you'll never open your heart and home to others. You'll miss out on flying high with the angels, meeting the cool people God strategically sends your way (each with a unique message of their own), touching lives and making a real difference.

Believe it or not, we hear "not until" excuses all the time, along with "when" promises. One lady we know, who used to drop by countless times for tea and an opportunity to chat, would continually say, "I'm having you over ... when I get my new tea set!" This went on for years, with no invites.

We eventually relocated to another area, too far for an easy commute, so our conversations have to be over the phone these days. Which is sad, because our friend missed her opportunity to extend hospitality, all because she was waiting for the "perfect time." It also beggars the question, "Did she ever get that new tea service?!?" The world may never know.

These excuses for avoiding the practice of hospitality are precisely that: *excuses*. None of the aforementioned concerns should ever become stumbling blocks to reaching out. Nothing—and we do mean *nothing*—needs to be perfect in order to extend hospitality. In fact, all that's truly necessary are an open heart and a willing spirit to be God's welcoming messenger of love and service.

So, we pray you'll avoid the pitfalls of perfectionism. Don't make excuses, don't wait for things to be perfect. Things probably never will be, and, thank God, they don't *need* to be!

If, however, you've mastered the art, and live in "a perfect house for entertaining," you're probably not making such excuses; by now, meeting the high standards set by the art may come quite naturally to you, and planning your next get-together will actually be fun, with no fear of failure. If so, that's a definite plus: you have an incredible skill set, and we pray you'll put it to good use in making people of all walks of life feel like the "angels" they are. But alas, you're in the minority.

Over the years, we've surveyed people from a wide variety of social, economic and ethnic backgrounds and age groups. Through our interviews with these men, women and young adults, we've made an amazing discovery. The vast majority of these folks do NOT want to be involved with the art of entertaining! That is, they don't mind being recipients of the benefits of the art, but they want nothing to do with the execution! (Was that Freudian?)

For brevity, we'll limit our discussion only to the findings of the ladies we surveyed, a diverse group of women, that included every type from homemaker to top business executive: first, modern entertaining, especially in the fashion of Martha Stewart, is NOT second nature to most women; in actuality, the vast majority of the ladies we interviewed admitted to feeling intimidated by the art of entertaining.

Second, for many of our interviewees, the subject of entertaining brought back bad memories and elicited more than a few frowns. No doubt because, as these women repeatedly stated, the whole idea of entertaining was a major source of S-T-R-E-S-S (!) in their lives.

Has the art of entertaining gotten so complicated and demanding that the average person fears to even attempt it? Have the "experts" raised the bar so high that few are able to meet the challenge? Does modern entertaining now require too much time and energy, as well as talents and resources many people simply don't have? Could it be that in trying to inspire people to entertain, Martha Stewart and her followers have inadvertently succeeded in discouraging the pursuit? We're sorry, but the answer to all these questions is a resounding YES!

But we can all breathe a sigh of relief, because, dear friends, there's another avenue to social interaction; a more excellent way, which has been around for thousands of years. It's the sacred practice of hospitality, and it's less complicated, less demanding, and hence, pretty much stress-free.

It's also less time-consuming and less expensive, because no one expects you to do what you can't, or share what you don't have. Like the caring grandmother we described in Chapter 3, you only use what you have on hand, but more importantly, you share from your heart!

Practicing hospitality can be so easy, so down-to-earth, and so much fun that once you've dipped a toe into the water, you'll soon find yourself taking the plunge. You'll be "hosting" in a relaxed atmosphere that will make guests feel comfortable *and* special—in *your* home, with *your* food, and everything done *your* way. No lofty standards, and no "testing" of your social skills. The only thing that will be on display is God's love shining through you!

Besides, when extending hospitality, you *should* be applying the "Unto Him Principal" we discussed in Chapter 3. Remember, all and any thing you do is done for an audience of One. He's the invisible Guest at every gathering. And *He* is certainly not demanding!

So please don't be misinformed: you don't have to know the art of entertaining to give a listening ear or a simple meal to someone who desperately needs a little TLC. We're all called to be God's messengers, but we needn't arrive bearing the same old message. Martha

Stewart brought *her* own unique message, the art of entertaining, at a time when the world needed it the most. She's an American Original, and no one can fill her shoes. Let's stop trying. What's *your* message? Is it one of love, hope and acceptance? We hope so!

God has commanded each of us to extend hospitality—not to be masters of the art of entertaining. He wants us to join His army of angels! In fact, He specifically wants YOU! That's right, wonderful, imperfect, one-of-a-kind YOU—*and not just an angel named Martha!*

CHAPTER 5:
STRAIGHT
FROM THE HEART!

Although we admire Martha Stewart for her many accomplishments, and can appreciate her message, we've never closely followed her. When it comes to the practice of hospitality, our role model is not a television personality. She is, however, something of a celebrity to us, and she predates Martha by a few decades. Today, at 81 years of age she's still reaching out, and still as hospitable as ever. Who is this unsung angel? None other than Wilma's mom, whom we affectionately call *Mamita*!

We plan to "visit" Mamita in another chapter, but at this point we'll simply note that she's been a true inspiration, and helped launch us into the practice of hospitality. We've lived out this sacred approach to social interaction throughout our thirty-two years of marriage, and we've learned numerous valuable insights about reaching angels from all walks of life. We've also thoroughly researched the subject, in both the Bible and external sources, and we've conducted countless interviews and surveys.

Last but not least, we've kept track of Martha Stewart, in order to be aware of each new trend in the secular pursuit of entertaining. What we've concluded from our studies, observations and experiences is: the ideal approach to social interaction is to incorporate the best aspects of the art of entertaining into the practice of hospitality.

We can use the ideas and skills of the art to create a pleasant and more inviting environment, or serve a meal in a way that's more colorful, fun and appetizing— whether we use fine China or pretty paper plates purchased from a "dollar store." Hence, the art of entertaining can become a satisfying way to enhance our efforts when extending hospitality. That is, as long as we avoid the pitfalls of the art, such as allowing its lofty standards to intimidate or lead to perfectionism.

As we discussed in the last chapter, striving to have everything perfect is the Holy Grail when pursuing the art. But during the practice of hospitality, we certainly don't want to go *there!* As discussed in Chapter 4, God has called us to pursue Excellence, not Perfectionism.

The Apostle Paul writes, "Don't copy the behavior and customs of this world, but let God transform you into a new person by changing the way you think. Then you will learn to know God's will for you, which is good and pleasing and perfect." (Romans 12:2 NLT) In other words, we believers should think, talk and behave differently from the rest of society. Hence, we need to avoid the pitfalls of the art of entertaining: *buying* and/or *doing* things in order to impress others, or to compete; becoming materialistic; and getting tangled up in perfectionism.

Use the art of entertaining if you wish, but never allow the art to control your thoughts and actions. Don't compare yourself to others, especially anyone who appears to have mastered the art. Just be yourself, the unique individual God created you to be, not a poor imitation of someone else! And don't waste your time and energy trying to keep up with the Joneses—or the Marthas. Instead, put these valuable commodities to better, more Godly use in obeying the Lord's commandment to "Love your neighbor." Above all, stop striving and stressing out in the pursuit of modern entertaining.

KEEP CALM and **PRACTICE BIBLICAL HOSPITALITY**

It's the antithesis of the "me, myself and I" mindset so prevalent today—because it's God-centered, and its focus is always on other people. The practice *can* (and often does) incorporate the positive elements of the art of entertaining, but it always shuns the negative aspects of its secular counterpart.

Furthermore, those who extend Biblical Hospitality are careful to remember that any and all their preparations are made solely to express genuine love, never to impress; no matter how festive the table looks, how delicious the food tastes, or how wonderful the decor of their homes, it's all intended to facilitate hospitality—to help guests feel welcome and extra special!

Like Martha Stewart, we too enjoy a bit of elegance and sophistication. It helps brighten the day, or evening, and can lend a touch of magic and romance to life. (Apparently we're not alone in our thinking, either, as evidenced by the tremendous popularity of the PBS television series *Downton Abbey*.) In fact, our personal style of hosting is actually more like Martha's, but ... We. Do *not*. Entertain!

We extend hospitality. And we enjoy many time-honored traditions, such as formal tea parties in the mode of Queen Victoria, which many today view as old-fashioned. But to quote Agent of S.H.I.E.L.D. Phil Coulson, in the movie *The Avengers,* "With everything that's happening ... people might just need a little old-fashioned."

Young adults certainly appreciate "a little old-fashioned." For instance, we used to host an annual formal dinner for the seniors at the local high school, and to make things really special we asked the young ladies to wear a nice dress or skirt, and the young men a shirt and tie—although some of the guys chose to add a sport coat for the dinner. If you could have seen how eagerly these students got into the swing of dressing up, and how much they enjoyed the sophistication of the affair, you'd really appreciate the "magic" of "old-fashioned"!

Hosting these graduating students was a true joy. And the little touches of elegance we incorporated into our gathering reassured these "angels" they were special and welcome in our home. So, "formal" doesn't have to be "stuffy," as long as your guests can sense your love.

It's actually possible to be formal *and* laid back. We recently hosted a young lady and her fiancée for dinner (both millennials), and the couple brought along their pooch. No problem, we love ... *pooches* (oh, and we never use the D-word). This was at Christmastime, and our home, Woodhaven, which is decorated and furnished in a Colonial American theme, was decked out with boughs of holly (*Fa la la la la, la la la lahh!*)—along with pineapples and red candles. The table was resplendent with our Winter Greetings China, and every seat was designated with a place-card held by a tiny cardinal. We love to dress up Woodhaven in all its Christmas finery!

Well, this couple walked in and immediately started with the *oohh*'s and *aahh*'s, as they tried to take in all the pretty decorations. And they continued to compliment us, on everything from the house to the food.

After dinner we sat in the living room, sang Christmas carols, and reminisced about God's many blessings throughout the year. Meanwhile, their pooch quickly got on Tom's lap to have his belly rubbed, before diplomatically moving on to Wilma's lap. Eventually, he found a corner of the sofa and started sleeping off his meal, dreaming, no doubt, about the broth we'd ladled onto his food. Yup, we supplied their pet with Christmas dinner, too; and yup, he was welcomed to relax on the Queen Anne sofa with our other guests.

We mention all this because near the close of the evening, the young lady commented, "Your house is so beautiful! It's formal—but not snooty! I feel so special!" And her fiancé was in complete agreement!

That one compliment meant more to us than anything else she could have said. Our taste in furnishings does lean to the formal—but it's what we enjoy, and it truly expresses who we are—but nothing is intended to impress, only to brighten the atmosphere. Above everything, we want our guests to feel at home, welcome and loved! And according to this lady, we apparently succeeded in our hospitality. *Woof!* Oh, and their pooch thought so, too.

Formal we may appear, but we also enjoy more casual fun, such as cookouts and ice cream socials. We really get "down home" whenever our Northern friends and family arrive from New York or New Jersey, serving them the "food of the gods": barbecue sandwiches topped with crispy Cole slaw, accompanied by hush puppies (told you we never use the D-word) and fresh banana pudding for dessert. *Mmmm-mmm!*

Sometimes we serve them Southern-fried chicken, with biscuits and gravy! And then we mustn't forget the delicious ... *Hey*, we'd better stop. We're making ourselves hungry. Plus, as we write this, we're both supposed to be on a d.i.e.t. (a four-letter word in our home). We will add, however, in the interest of full disclosure, that we don't personally prepare these delicacies.

We live about twenty minutes from two "gourmet" markets that fry up some mean chicken every day; and we're also not far from a family-operated business that weekly smokes and daily cooks out-of-this-world barbecue! We've enjoy their food for over three decades, and when we bring it home to serve our Northern friends, it's a sight to watch them *chow down*! (We were going to write "pig out," but decided to avoid the obvious pun.) Suffice to say, our guests truly enjoy this divine yet down-to-earth fare.

The Adventure of the Satanic Sofa!

During our thirty-two years of practicing Biblical Hospitality, the Lord has brought many "angels" into our lives, people who have needed and received our TLC, and who have also shared from their own hearts.

These angels we've welcomed into our home have come from many walks of life; they've had different faiths, or no faith at all; they widely vary in ethnicity and nationality, education and social status; and they range in age from infancy to the well-seasoned nineties. They've brought their cats, dogs and, believe it or not, even their birds. Yes indeed, we've hosted a song bird for a weekend, and dined on tacos with a lady and her cockatiel.

What do all these guests have in common? Friend or fowl, all these visitors need the same thing to remain healthy and happy: the most powerful source of "energy" in the Universe—no, not that glowing cube in *The Avengers*—God's supernatural love! Furthermore, even as we write this, there is someone somewhere who desperately needs this source of love, hope and acceptance—which can only flow through you and your expressions of hospitality. He or she might be someone you pass each day, and yet fail to see; or a person you've yet to meet, a person who can benefit from a cup of tea and a listening ear.

These "messengers" each have a story to relate, and need a welcoming environment in which to share it. We can reach out and help them with our own personal message of God's love, and in return, be greatly blessed by what these angels can share with us. We've done this as a married couple since the early 1980s. It's been an incredible journey and, believe us, we've come a long way.

After we first got married we lived in the next-to-the-last house on a dead-end road. It was a modest rented rancher filled with mismatched secondhand furniture and decorated only with faded hand-me-down drapes. Nothing about these arrangements reflected our style or our dreams of the future. But, hey, it was home!

We were content with everything God had given us, happy, grateful—and very much in love. (And still are!)

Our first "new" sofa was the stuff of legends, a true classic in every sense. It belonged to our Pastor, who'd gotten it used when a member of his church decided the thing had seen better days. Our pastor had held on to it for a couple of years, until the Lord decided to maketh His servant lie down in green pastures and sitteth on softer cushions. At which time, when we heard our pastor was about to put the sofa out by the curb, we immediately asked for it. He graciously gave us this tired old beast of frayed fabric and broken springs, while trying unsuccessfully to conceal a baffled look of surprise and pity.

But, as goes the saying "one man's junk is another man's treasure," we were thrilled to get to this new (um, newish ... uh, not *that* old) sofa for our sparsely furnish- ed living room!

Once we'd carried this "treasure" into our home and sat on it for two minutes, we realized why our Pastor had thought it best to put the thing out by the curb! One end of the sofa was so broken-down that when you sat on it you'd start to sink into the cushions, as though you were being swallowed up by the beast. At the other end—Pardon the pun! (*Oh?* You don't understand why this is a pun? Read on.)—at the *other* end, an evil spring found devious new ways to keep us on our toes!

So we instantly made a solemn pact: we knew that we could never *ever* allow a guest to suffer at the coils of the beast. No, whenever visitors called, we'd give them the best seats in the house, while we'd sit on our satanic sofa, always with furrowed brows and forced smiles upon our tortured faces. *Selah!*

Did our humble home and "eccentric" furnishings keep us from extending hospitality? Of course not! Were we ashamed to open our door to guests who lived in bigger and better houses "perfect for entertaining"? Nope! Were we embarrassed to serve meals on cheap Corelle dishes instead of fine china? Not at all. Do you know why? No, it *wasn't* because "misery loves company"! In fact, we didn't even think about our house and furniture. Why should we? "Home is where the *heart* is!" And *love* is the key to the front door—nothing else matters when practicing hospitality. It certainly didn't to us, and we hope it won't matter to you!

In addition to having less than the "perfect home" in those days, we also struggled with time and "talents." We never had a lot of extra cash on hand, or spare time. We both worked long hours, one of us as a high school teacher, the other as a chemist for a large company. We spent a good deal of whatever time remained serving in our local church. Among other things, we prepared Bible studies, conducted MasterLife classes, wrote articles for a Christian newspaper, and ... led the pony rides during the church carnival. And yet, we found time—excuse us—we *made* time to extend hospitality to various people we encountered.

Time and money are only small factors in the *hospitality equation*, however, and we need <u>The God Factor</u> to solve this equation! God has a way of multiplying our resources. He can greatly add to our most meager efforts, giving us fresh ideas for expressing His love, making dollars stretch, and helping us properly divide our time between everyday demands and His sacred command. God is both a master chef and the ultimate accountant—as when He gave us the idea, during our lean years, for baked ziti using spam! (So delicious, we still make it occasionally!)

Today we have a nice house in the woods filled with books, and surrounded by beasts and birds. We also have attractive and comfortable furniture, and other pretty things which reflect our style and personality. But it took years of saving money, searching out sales, and buying one piece at a time. We didn't mind, however; we turned furnishing our home into an adventure, hunting bargains, making deals and trading coupons with the natives. And to this day, we struggle with paying the full price for most stuff. Just about everything we have has a story connected to it. Every piece is a trophy of a wild expedition to bag a ferocious bargain!

In this way, each our furnishings comes with its own unique message. Yes, our house is filled with inanimate "angels"! In the dining room, a stuffed peacock named Darcy greets guests from his perch atop a corner curio (—named for the character in *Pride and Prejudice*) as he surveys his domain, which includes a dining room set that eagerly points he's a wedding gift from our Mamita! Elsewhere in Woodhaven, other messengers await, praising the goodness of God while harboring secrets of scandalous savings! Many of these angels also testify to the kindness and generosity of friends and family, especially "big" sister Wanda.

No we're not crazy. A little loony, perhaps, but not crazy. (If we had more money we could call ourselves eccentric.) We simply have fun naming the things we frequently use and depend upon, and giving voice to the lessons these objects can teach. We even wrote a book, *Angel in the Kitchen,* in which we share such teachings as the spiritual significance of Tupperware, why people are like eggs, and what happens when the cheese stands alone!

All this is intended to explain how much and precisely why we love Woodhaven! And yet, Woodhaven is not the "perfect house for entertaining"—nor does it need to be. It's warm and inviting, but it doesn't come equipped with all the latest features so popular in those HGTV shows we previously mentioned. But what our wonderful home lacks in material perfection, we make up for … with love. Like grandma's humble home, and perhaps even yours, our Woodhaven is filled with God's love, hope and grace. It may not be perfect for entertaining, but it's the absolute best place to extend hospitality.

One last thought before we move on: houses really *are* like people. They can be very welcoming despite their faults. Furthermore, would you hesitate to introduce us to a good friend just because that person isn't "perfect"? Who is? Nor would you keep a family member shut away in an attic room, so don't shut up your home either! Introduce your "castle" to the world, through the practice of hospitality!

Heart to Heart!

Friends, we've shared these personal experiences and details not to say, "Hey, look at us!" But rather to make a vital point. The Lord has freed us from the bonds of entertaining, and He longs to do the same for you. He's also charged us with a precious message to bring to light the misconceptions surrounding the sacred practice of hospitality, which have led to its neglect and even abandonment. And He wants all His people to understand that this neglect has dire consequences for our families, communities and places of work and worship—because the sacred practice is the cement for building and strengthening relationships, the most important thing in life!

We also want you to understand that what we're sharing is not head knowledge. It flows from decades of experiences, because we've lived out the practice of hospitality throughout our marriage. Hence, we've witnessed firsthand the power of God's sacred practice to impact the lives of those around us. No, our message comes straight from the heart!

We've seen how a simple meal can communicate hope and acceptance to a weary or wayward soul who feels unworthy of God's love. (By the way, who among us actually *is* worthy? And yet God dishes out His love anyway! So, as believers, shouldn't we follow *His* example?) We've also realized that a prompting from the Lord to reach out to a neighbor over a cup of coffee can end up in prayer for an illness nobody else knows about; or that sharing a tuna sandwich with a new coworker can start that person down the road to forgiveness and eventually marital reconciliation!

When extending hospitality, the possibilities for making a difference in the world are limitless, which is why we want to encourage you to open your heart and home to the people God sends your way. Once you make yourself available to the Lord, He will do AMAZING things through you, as He blesses the lives of those you touch with His love! And God will also bless you, in ways you cannot imagine—as His special angel!

But how can God accomplish such great things using *me* in such a simple way? Easy. The Apostle Paul writes, "God chose the foolish things of the world to shame the wise; God chose the weak things of the world to shame the strong." (1 Corinthians 1:27 NIV) God actually chose flawed people like you and us to do the seemingly impossible through seemingly foolish means!

This is a truth God's servants have relied on for 2,000 years. TBN founders Paul and Jan Crouch often pointed to this truth whenever someone asked how they managed to build a single television station into the world's largest Christian Broadcasting Network, reaching millions of people across the globe. In fact, after her beloved went home to be with the Father, Jan simply stated, "We didn't build it! [The Lord] did!"

And yet, despite some views, the practice of hospitality is no fool's errand. To the contrary, it's a sacred practice, a divine directive, and a Biblical command. It's a practice that's near and dear to God's heart. Actually, it's the single practice that's most representative of God's heart, because after all, our Lord is loving, giving and welcoming! He came to earth as a servant (Philippians 2:7) and ultimately invited all those who follow Him to become a part of God's family! Sounds pretty hospitable, right?

Our definition of *hospitality*, an attitude of the heart (love) expressed through a lifestyle of giving and serving, actually describes the life of Christ. Although we can't delve into Jesus' hospitable lifestyle here, we will point out a few interesting facts about His life which illustrate that He's the ultimate example for the sacred practice.

- Our Lord loves gatherings and celebrations of all kinds. In fact, holidays (*holy* days set apart to commemorate and celebrate special occasions) were His invention! And, specifically what we Gentiles call the "Jewish Holidays" are especially personal to God. "And the Lord spoke to Moses, saying, 'Speak to the children of Israel, and say to them: *The Feasts of the Lord,*[2] *which you shall proclaim to be holy convocations, these are My feasts.'"* (Leviticus 23:1-2 NKJV)

- Jesus performed His first miracle at a wedding in Cana, when He turned water into wine. (John 2:1-12) It's no coincidence His *first* miracle was tied to God's *first* institution.

- The *last* event in human history is called "The Marriage Supper of the Lamb." (Revelation 9:19) At this cosmic event all of His followers from throughout the ages will partake in the greatest celebration of all time. We can hardly wait!

- Jesus said, "...Whoever wishes to become great among you, he will be your servant; ...even as the Son of Man did not come to be served, but to serve, and to give His life as a ransom for many." (Matthew 20:26, 28 Berean Literal)

- Jesus' preoccupation with hospitality actually drew criticism from the religious leaders of His day—in the form of snide remarks. "The Son of Man came eating and drinking, and they say, 'Look at him! A glutton and a drunkard, a friend of tax collectors and sinners!'" (Matthew 11:19 ESV) In other words, Jesus was (and remains) welcoming and inclusive of everyone; and He frequently broke bread with people from the wrong side of the tracks!

- Jesus was (and remains) an excellent host, a truth He demonstrated when He threw the biggest picnic the world has ever known: motivated

---

[2] For further reading, please refer to the Endnotes: The Feasts of Lord: Resources, on page 191.

by compassion for a hungry multitude, Jesus miraculously multiplied a basketful of fishes and loaves to feed "5,000 men and their families." (Mark 6:35-44 NLT) In fact, He did this not once, but twice! (See also Matthew 15:32-39) Thus, the miracles involving the largest number of people had to do with hospitality!

God's practice of hospitality is all about relationships. From the beginning, God has demonstrated all the aspects of the practice. He created us specifically to have a close personal relationship with Him; and later He came in the form of a man to reconcile and build upon that relationship. He did so as the ultimate act of love, expressed through a life of giving and serving. (There's our definition, again.) We'll discuss this topic more in another chapter, but for now, we'll simply leave you with this:

NEWSFLASH: *Our Lord, the God of Abraham, Isaac, and Israel, is above all else a HOSPITABLE GOD! And His one purpose for each of us is that we become like Him! Our Heavenly Father longs for a people of hospitality. In truth, God's followers should be the most loving, accepting, and welcoming people on the planet.*

Oh, yeah, and as Lieutenant Columbo would often say between puffs on his cigar, "There's just one more thing." You probably already know this, but it bears repeating: if you're a follower of God, everything you are and everything you have belongs to *Him!* Your time, talents and money; your house, whether modest like ours or "perfect for entertaining"; and everything in it; all "your" possessions belong to God. He entrusts them to you as a way of blessing you in this life, but still, you're simply the steward of all God's resources here on earth.

Relax. God's loaned you all this stuff because He loves you, and He wants you to make full use of it. Of course, He expects you to use it in the right way—and to share it, too! In fact, God plainly states "...You shall not harden your heart or shut your hand against your poor brother.... You shall give to him freely, and your heart shall not be grudging when you give to him, because for this the LORD your God will bless you in all your work and in all that you undertake." (Deuteronomy 15:7, 10 ESV) In a nutshell (taking into consideration our status as His stewards, along with the hospitable nature of God), our Lord expects each and every one of us to practice hospitality.

Now comes the clincher. Even YOU belong to God! And, as with the rest of God's stuff, your time, talent and resources—excuse us, *God's* time, talent and resources—our Lord expects you to share who you are with those around you. But you can't do this if you're keeping your house and heart shut up to others. You have to join the rest of us angels, by being God's hands extended; by practicing hospitality.

As we've continually stated, the sacred practice goes far beyond sharing your time and money; its ultimate expression happens when we give of ourselves. Offering our companionship, sharing who we are, and letting people know that we really care, all these things communicate God's love best of all, and encompass the divine message of hospitality. Such things also reveal the true heart of an angel.

For those who've confused the practice of hospitality with modern entertaining, who've discounted its importance, delegated it to others, and made up lame excuses for personally avoiding it, the facts of God's sacred practice may come as a shock. But our purpose is not to shock you, or to shame you. We merely want you to know the truth, because "...The truth will set you free." (John 8:32 NIV)

Take hold of the truth of hospitality, and you'll be free from the constraints of the art of entertaining; free from feeling inadequate; free from comparing yourself to others; free from competing; free from the stress of trying to keep up with the Jones, or the Marthas; and free from the bondage of perfectionism.

You'll also be free to do what God's calling you to do, reaching out to others, touching lives, building relationships, making a difference ... all through simple but practical expressions of God's love and acceptance. You'll be free to fly with the angels, and that's all the Lord desires—and everything we could hope for. It's our message to you, and it comes straight from the heart!

CHAPTER 6:
WHAT THE
ANGELS KNOW!

If you happen to be someone who enjoys the art of entertaining, and feel like we're raining on your parade, you can take heart. That's the last thing we want to do.

As we stated earlier, there's nothing inherently wrong with the art, or enjoying the elegance of more elaborate gatherings. And we'll be the first to admit that the art serves an important purpose in our society. For instance, many professionals and government officials use the art to enhance their business meetings or political functions.

Depending on the size, these gatherings might take place in a home, a restaurant, or a banquet hall; but nearly always, the services or facilities used are provided by a person or company associated with the "hospitality industry" which, like the art, also plays an important role today.

Company Christmas parties, retirement dinners, wedding receptions, anniversary celebrations and other special events are all occasions during which the art of entertaining may be on full display. A community picnic, a church cookout, and regional food festivals are all part of entertaining. So, entertaining (and its art) does not have to be formal or stressful. Indeed, these social activities are actually fun—and we could use many more of these events. Truth be told, at a time when people are becoming insular and isolated from others, when often the only "families" they see are the ones in television sitcoms, any activity that brings people together is greatly appreciated.

In an age when many people interact only on social media, and the only "friends" they have are on Facebook, anything that promotes face-to-face contact with our fellow travelers in life is a good thing! And in a world where many have become socially inept, feeling awkward around others, and more comfortable *texting* than *talking* on their phones, or, heaven forbid, holding a conversation one-to-one, any endeavor that encourages human contact and real social interaction—no matter what its flaws might be—is a big step in the right direction.

We may not be into entertaining, but we can still recognize its role in today's world. Similarly, we're not followers of Martha Stewart, but we still appreciate what she can bring to the table (both literally and figuratively speaking) with the art of entertaining. And we acknowledge that to Martha's credit, she and her many imitators have together inspired millions of women (and men) to master the art and follow in their footsteps.

Some of the consequences of this movement toward the art have been negative. But on the other hand, some have been beneficial: prompting people to share their crafts, culinary gifts, and beautiful homes with others.

If you've ever had the privilege of knowing someone like Martha Stewart, who's mastered the art of entertaining, and been invited to one of his or her social events, then you know how special such an event can be. When properly executed, the art can provide a real treat. After all, who doesn't enjoy a gourmet meal served on an exquisite table in a beautiful dining room? We certainly don't mind getting the royal treatment! Hey, Martha, can we come to your house the next time you entertain? Pretty please?

Unless you skipped over the first five chapters of this book, you know we'd rather have people practicing hospitality than pursuing the art of entertaining. Hospitality is a more excellent way to social interaction. However, modern entertaining, like so many other secular things in the world, has its own merits. It reminds us of the current popularity of superhero movies: although we love faith-based films that inspire us to grow in Christ, we have to confess that Captain America, Nick Fury, and the rest of the Avengers are at the top of our list of cinema favorites. *Pass the popcorn!*

Our point is, not everything of a secular nature is wrong—including modern entertaining—as long as it doesn't violate God's Word or undermine what our Lord is trying to accomplish. Hence, as long as the art of entertaining doesn't impede the practice of hospitality, there's room for both the sacred practice *and* its secular counterpart. Some people have absolutely no problem balancing both—but many people *do.*

We occasionally meet individuals who can incorporate the best aspects of the art to reach out to others, who understand that in practicing hospitality there's more at stake than having a good time or pulling off a "perfect" event. This tiny category of people use the art to open the lines of communication and build relationships, to meet with the "angels" and touch hearts.

But in reality, the majority who dabble in the art are confused and frustrated, and their association with this secular pursuit has resulted in violating God's Word—to the neglect of His sacred command and the detriment of His divine purpose for His people. Chasing after the art has consumed them!

Jesus said, "Render to Caesar the things that are Caesar's, and to God the things that are God's." (Mark 12:17 NASB) His statement was made in regard to paying taxes, but we can apply the underlying truth to many situations in life. If we owe a debt (money, gratitude, or credit for accomplishing something beneficial) then we certainly should give it. And so, we officially give the art of entertaining its due. Like so many things in the secular world, it has its value. That said, however, we must also point out that many people (including those within the Body of Christ) are rendering to "Caesar" a lot more than he's due!

As our society moves further away from the Judeo-Christian principles upon which it was founded, it's easy to lose track of the true Biblical origins, values and motivations behind many of the ideas and activities that now seem commonplace. We've done this in the case of social interaction: we've given the art of entertaining far more credit than it's due, and we've lost sight of the spiritual reasons behind reaching out to others. In other words, as our culture moved closer to the pursuit of modern entertaining, the concept of hospitality got left behind!

We previously discussed the importance of gaining a Heavenly perspective on the sacred practice. And this is certainly the viewpoint traditionally held by the Jewish people. According to author Rabbi Joseph

Telushkin, "...Hospitality is not just a social nicety, [as most people believe today,] but a serious moral and legal obligation." (*Jewish Literacy*, p. 534)

For God's Chosen People, who've faithfully honored the mandates of their Creator despite thousands of years of persecution, and who continue to observe the tremendously important "Feasts of the Lord" (Please see Chapter 5), hospitality has always been (and continues to be) *front and center* to everyday life!

Telushkin writes that while Jewish hospitality is the norm, "...Inhospitality, on the other hand, is not simply ungracious behavior but vile and absolutely forbidden"! (p. 534) We could learn a great deal about social interaction from our "Hebrew" brothers and sisters, both past and present. But regarding our ideas about God's sacred practice, we *definitely* need to return to the Jewish roots of our faith!

Today, what most people think of as hospitality is actually its secular substitute. They've been so confused by Western culture and popular trends that when they *think* they're extending hospitality to their boss or sweet Aunt Matilda, they're really just entertaining. That's fine—for what it is, a wonderful occasion where every-thing is picture perfect and people have fun; but it falls woefully short of accomplishing the work of the angels. It's not getting to change lives, and it will be quickly forgotten as soon as the next "big event" rolls around.

The art of entertaining has its place in society. When properly used, it can enhance the practice of hos-pitality. But the art itself, along with the secular pursuit of modern entertaining, lacks the spiritual component necessary to minister to people and build relation-ships—we are, after all, spiritual and relational beings.

Entertaining lacks the power to go beyond the superficial aspects of life. It is a social nicety consisting of good food and social mingling, anchored in the temporal realm, and hence, it does nothing to foster spiritual growth, produce significant change, or effect eternal consequences.

The secular pursuit of entertaining has, however, created a great deal of confusion concerning the practice of hospitality, resulting in people misunderstanding God's spiritual concept, and therefore wanting nothing to do with it.

Biblical Hospitality is an attitude of the heart (love) expressed through a lifestyle of serving and giving (of one's time, talents and resources—but most importantly, of oneself). It's a commandment and a divine directive, to be carried out in practical ways that open doors of communication, build bridges to unity, foster meaningful relationships, promote healing, and touch lives on a spiritual level and with eternal consequences. It's the sacred practice of angels!

Unintended Consequences

Oftentimes in life, what starts out as a good idea, or a noble pursuit with the best intentions, can end in disaster. Noble pursuits can derail, and good ideas can lead the way to unintended consequences. This is precisely what happened with the art of entertaining: Martha Stewart (and others who followed the trail she blazed) had the best of intentions. She wanted to inspire people to open their homes and enjoy the company of guests, and she wanted them to have fun doing so, by introducing artistic (and often elaborate) aspects and elements that would allow people to indulge their creativity. But the creative aspects, along with the idea of doing things with style and artistic flair, ultimately proved to be too much for the average person.

Martha's good intentions actually paved the way to a dramatic drop in the number of people willing to entertain; and the art of entertaining crashed with so much force it nearly destroyed the Biblical concept of hospitality. We state this with authority. Of the diverse group of people we surveyed during months of interviews, most of them want nothing to do with the art, and as a result of their bad experiences and confusion, only a small remnant still open their homes to guests.

Ironically, the art of entertaining is its own worst enemy. By its very nature as an art, it leads to a weird process of natural selection: as the saying goes, "Only the strong survive"; and this was never more true than in this secular pursuit. Those few brave souls who've mastered the art, and who have enough confidence to enter the arena of modern entertaining, are still standing. But as we look around "the coliseum" we also see the ground littered with those who have fallen, the victims of the lion-sized demands of the art.

As we discussed in Chapter 4, the excesses of entertaining, with its high standards, its obsession with getting everything perfect, and its resultant stress, are too much for most folks. The art may consume some people, but others it devours!

The vast majority of people have found entertaining to be so demanding, so challenging, so expensive, so time-consuming, so nerve wracking, and therefore so intimidating, they react to the pursuit the same way most of us would react to an IRS tax audit! With sheer undisguised, unadulterated ... *PANIC!!* First, they don't feel up to the "ordeal"! Second, they fear their social skills and cooking abilities won't correctly "add up"; or that their ignorance of etiquette and less than "perfect" home will upset their guests—whom they perceive as being there *only* to audit their performance. And the bottom line? People realize they have to file tax returns, but they don't have to entertain. So they don't.

Are these people overreacting? Uh, *no!* The art of entertaining **focuses** on externals: the house, the food, the table settings, and all the other paraphernalia needed to pull off a perfect gathering, and indeed, everything *must* be perfect. And when it comes to the art, it doesn't matter if your heart's in the right place; what *does* matter is whether or not the silverware's in the right place!

PEOPLE and their emotional needs are never important in entertaining. Not to worry, though, the people will still come for the "show"! Excuse us, *dinner* and a show, because you cannot entertain without food! Can you imagine Martha having someone over just to listen to and pray about his or her troubles?

No, there's gotta be food. It plays a major role. It should be gourmet. And served with panache. Oh, and never talk with your mouth full!

Unlike modern entertaining, the practice of hospitality does not necessarily require food. It's always a good idea to provide your guests with physical sustenance—we personally never want people to leave Woodhaven hungry—but there are times when hospitality takes other forms, such as praying with a friend, or driving a shut-in neighbor to a doctor's appointment, or ... just being there for someone! Such hospitable acts constitute what our Jewish friends call a *mitzvah!*

"A mitzvah," writes Steve Herzig in *Jewish Culture & Customs*, "is a command given by God; it is a divine precept. The definition has been expanded to include anything that promotes proper behavior. [It] has also been translated to mean *charity* ... [or a] *good deed*." (p. 46) So the practice of hospitality clearly goes hand in hand with the concept of the *mitzvah*.

The Apostle Paul understood the importance of being hospitable through the mitzvah. He said, "I have given you an example that ... we should help the weak. We should remember the words that the Lord Jesus said, 'Giving gifts is more satisfying than receiving them.'" (Acts 20:35 GOD'S WORD)

Herzig further states, "...Many Jewish people believe that performing a mitzvah is a means of ... providing great personal satisfaction in doing *the right thing*." (p. 46) Whether we call it performing a mitzvah or practicing hospitality, one thing's certain: from a Heavenly perspective, expressing God's love through thoughtful acts of giving and serving is always *the right thing* to do!

Samuel Says!

In the practice of hospitality, the **focus** is on *people*, not *things*—and the unseen internal matters of the heart, such as love, hope and acceptance. Nothing needs to be perfect, because it's NOT an art. It's reaching out, while simply being yourself, to make people feel comfortable and welcome. And if you serve food, it doesn't have to be a gourmet meal served on fancy dishes.

If you're a good cook, then excellent—your guests are in for a treat. But it's just as hospitable to serve a sandwich on a paper plate, as long as you do it as an act of sincere kindness. You can serve a slice of take-out pizza, or a cup of chicken noodle soup zapped for two minutes in the microwave, as long as do it in love. In fact, Proverbs 15:17 states, "Better to have a dish of vegetables where there is love, than a juicy steak where there is hate." (GOD'S WORD)

But again, by its very definition, you can extend hospitality *without* serving food. In fact, when it comes to the sacred practice—to quote the Beatles song—"all you need is love," because *nothing* is as important as the people we can reach through hospitality.

Let's restate this, for the sake of clarity: no *thing* is as important as the people who are the **focus** of hospitality. The food we might serve, or the soft music playing in the background, the pretty plates or the colorful tablecloth are simply some of the many tools we might use to reach people.

Think about this: it's 5:30 p.m., and you've just left work. You're tired, hungry and you want to get home. Up ahead there's a police officer directing rush-hour traffic at a busy intersection. His main concern is meeting your need to get home—in one piece. To meet *your* needs and accomplish *his* purpose for being there, he may use a number of methods and several pieces of equipment.

What's most important to this public servant? That he look nice in his uniform as he waves his white-gloved hands? Or that his shiny new whistle glints in the light of the early evening sun? Or that he blows that whistle like a trumpet player at a concert? *Hmm.* What would *you* want our traffic-directing friend to be most concerned about?

When extending hospitality, we're not unlike the guy standing in the flow of human traffic. Our one concern is to express love in a practical way, by meeting the needs of others. How we go about accomplishing this is up to us. What we use is up to us, and will depend only on the needs of the people we want to reach, and the resources available to us. Our "whistles" and other equipment might look old and tarnished, but as long as they get the job done, it's not a big deal. "Better a small tarnished whistle that gets you through traffic, than a big polished tuba that causes an accident!" (Proverbs ... No, we're just kidding!)

When extending hospitality, it's important to remember what the Prophet Samuel states, "The LORD doesn't see things the way you see them. People judge by outward appearance, but the LORD looks at the heart." (1 Samuel 16:7 NLT) In other words, *what* people do, and *why* they do it, are more important to God than how they look while they're doing it! Therefore, in Biblical Hospitality, as long as your heart is motivated by love, your efforts will always make the grade! Whatever you do, no matter how simple, will always be appreciated by both the Lord *and* those who need a little TLC.

1 Samuel 16:7 also leads us to another point: if we want to be more godly, we can no longer judge a book (or anything else, for that matter) by its cover. For example, beneath the cover of grandma's faded and frayed tea cozy, probably lies a hearty pot of Earl Grey brewed with lots of love!

When it comes to hospitality (whether extending it or receiving it), we must look beyond the humble home (ours or someone else's), beyond ethnicity, or economic and social status (ours or theirs), and beyond trifling externals. Once we start viewing people through God's eyes of love, we'll quickly recognize them for what they are, His angels on earth! We'll also become more caring and sensitive to their needs.

Try to keep God's perspective regarding people and things, and you really can't go wrong. Practice hospitality in love, and even your most humble efforts will rate as triumphs! Obey this sacred command, in the way you're most comfortable with, and God will number you—yes, unique and wonderful YOU—among His messengers of love!

So, you see? There's *absolutely* NO pressure. Now repeat after us: "What, *me* worry?"

Paying the Price

Despite decades of watching Martha Stewart and her celebrity imitators performing the art of entertaining on television; despite books, magazines, and DVDs crammed with well-intended advice; despite an entire line of Martha Stewart signature products to aid the novice in modern entertaining; despite the availability of prepared foods at gourmet markets; despite the new take-out services offered by upscale restaurants; despite the increasing number of catering businesses; despite the fact that the average American now has more leisure time and disposable income than ever before in the history of our country ... fewer and fewer people are entertaining.

The business of promoting entertaining is bigger than ever—in fact, it's a multi-billion dollar industry—and yet, those who "consume" all the stuff about the art hardly ever use it. But hey, we get it. People also love to watch crime shows on TV, but how many of us are going out to rob a bank? Apparently, most consumers view all the stuff about entertaining as, well, entertainment: fun to watch, but who's crazy enough to try it?

This mass exodus from actually being involved in modern entertaining has greatly impacted the practice of hospitality, as well. We began our discussion of God's sacred command by stating it's one of the most neglected and misunderstood concepts in our society today. The biggest misconception is that it's the same thing as entertaining, an art mastered by the few. As previously explained: *not even.*

Unfortunately, most people remain uninformed of the truth of Biblical Hospitality. They think they know what it is, having seen or heard all about it; and not liking what they've seen or heard, they've walked away from this vital spiritual endeavor. But in actuality, few have witnessed the real deal in action. Sure, they've probably had ringside seats for various bouts of entertaining, maybe felt the stress of the host or hostess, and were perhaps even tagged by the demands of the art themselves. But they've yet to see God's champ in action, because very few practice genuine hospitality these days.

Thanks to the unintended *negative* consequences of Martha Stewart's well-intentioned approach to social interaction, we're all paying the price: people have been turned off by the art of entertaining, and they've tuned out. But in their confusion, they've also tuned out anything to do with Biblical Hospitality. To paraphrase the old proverb, they've thrown out God's precious baby with the dirty bath water!

It's no big deal if you don't want to entertain. As we stated earlier, we don't entertain, either. After all, entertaining is just a social nicety of no eternal consequence. We do, however, extend hospitality, and that's a whole 'nother thing! It's a divine directive mandated by God, and not practicing it can have serious ramifications: first, a failure to extend hospitality will greatly affect an individual's relationship with God. Because *if* we love God, we keep His commands, right?

The Apostle John writes, "...We can be sure that we know Him if we obey His commandments. ....Those who obey God's Word truly show how completely they love Him. That is how we know we are living in Him." (1 John 2:5 NLT)

Second, it affects our relationships with those around us. How can we love our neighbor when we don't even take the proper steps to get to know the person? Truth is, we really can't; at least, not in the way God intends us. Which is why Romans 12:13 reminds us, "Always be eager to practice hospitality." (NLT)

We *told* you hospitality was all about relationships! And relationships are the most important thing in life. Put these two inescapable facts together and you come up with but one unavoidable conclusion.

We can retreat from the secular art of entertaining, but each and everyone one of us must take part in the Biblical practice of hospitality. We must do so in order to be obedient; to love God and strengthen our relationship with Him; to connect with those around us, first getting to know our "neighbor," so that we can then fully love him or her as God intended, through practical expressions of giving and serving; thereby fulfilling BOTH requirements of the Greatest Commandment, to "love God" and "love your neighbor as yourself." (Matthew 27:37-40)

Dear reader, the last thing we want to do is lay a guilt trip on you. But the Lord has called us to be messengers of truth, and the truth we bring is this: if you're not already doing so, then you need to obey God's command to practice hospitality by opening your heart and home to others.

But *please*, never do it out of a sense of obligation. Do it out of love for God—and the people He created in His own image! Do it because it's right. Do it because it fosters relationships. Do it because it's what this world needs now more than ever before!

One need not be a prophet or a sociologist or even a psychologist to realize relationships are vital to every civilized society as well as to the mental health of all individuals. Strong meaningful relationships strengthen families and communities, and promote unity, harmony and order. But over the last few decades, the importance of relationships has been overlooked in a mad dash to get ahead in life. The current high rate of divorce and the deterioration of the nuclear family are the most obvious proofs of this.

Pastor Matthew Hagee, in a recent sermon, offered a further bit of proof that relationships are souring, stating "Kindness is an endangered species!" He then added, "Instead of people opening the door for someone, they'll elbow their way to get in front of them!" Whatever happened to being hospitable? Well, that's the problem. We've neglected the sacred practice, and our relationships are suffering for it!

We're not prophets of gloom and doom. Neither is the sky falling ... yet. But we do need to work on our relationships. Although there's a remnant still reaching out by practicing hospitality, the world desperately needs more angels to step up to the plate. We *can* turn these trends around. It will take time, and it won't be easy but, as an angel of the Lord spoke to Mary—yeah, this time we mean *angel* as an actual celestial being— "...Nothing is impossible for God." (Luke 1:37 GOD'S WORD)

If we return to God and the truth of His Word, and commit to obeying His command to practice hospitality, we can make this world a much brighter place. We'll still have our share of problems, and life will never be perfect—this is, after all, planet earth, not Heaven—but we'll be taking positive steps to carry out God's will. And through His sacred practice we'll be better able to interact socially; we'll be able to pull down the walls that divide us, open the lines of communication, and build and nurture the kind of relationships that bring healing and unity.

In fact, we honestly believe that many of the issues we face in our communities and places of work and worship, as well as the problems we struggle with in our homes, can ultimately be resolved over a meal at the kitchen table!

Does this sound naïve or too simplistic? We have sufficient Biblical and historical evidence to make you a believer, not to mention decades of personal experience in which we've seen firsthand the power of hospitality to impact people in a positive and life-changing way. We'll examine some of this evidence as we continue to peel away the many layers of the hospitality "onion."

The Apostle Paul wrote, in his letter to the believers living in the sprawling, decadent city of Rome, "Don't just pretend to love others. Really love them. Hate what is wrong. Hold tightly to what is good. Love each other with genuine affection, and take delight in honoring each other. Never be lazy, but work hard and serve the Lord enthusiastically. ...When God's people are in need, be ready to help them. Always be eager to practice hospitality. Do all that you can to live in peace with every one ... If your enemies are hungry, feed them. If they are thirsty, give them something to drink. ...Don't let evil conquer you, but conquer evil by doing good." (Romans 12:9-11, 13, 18, 20-21 NLT)

Paul clearly understood the importance of hospitality in reaching out to the Romans. And things aren't that different today. The times and circumstances may change, but people rarely do. We *need* to return to the practice of hospitality *en masse*, and as soon as possible. It's a divine directive for all of God's *messengers* here on earth; the key to opening doors and touching lives in a lost world, and the secret to building and strengthening relationships.

These sobering truths about hospitality are what the angels know!

CHAPTER **7**:
MEN, WOMEN, & ANGELS

Guys and gals ... as different as night and day, cats and dogs, salt and pepper? In his 1993 book on human relationships, *Men are from Mars, Women are from Venus*, John Gray suggested men and women are so drastically different that one might imagine they originated from two distinct worlds. But how does the Creator of the Universe view the genders?

Gray's book drew some serious criticism during the 1990s, for reinforcing gender stereotypes. One of its many critics is Erina MacDonald, a Purdue University communications professor, who conducted a survey of men and women in 2004, using questionnaires and interviews. Professor MacDonald found that the sexes are not so different after all, but "books like John Gray's ... tell men that being masculine means dismissing feelings and downplaying problems. That isn't what most men do, and it isn't good for either men or women."

Well, despite its numerous and vocal critics, Gray's book sold over 50 million copies, making it one of the best-selling nonfiction works of all time. So obviously, *somebody* liked the book. In fact, for years we frequently heard Gray's book referenced in various conversations. These allusions to his work usually went something like this: in the midst of a disagreement, often between a married couple, one stubborn spouse would inevitably shrug and say, "Too bad! Men are from Mars, Women are from Venus!" It sounded like a cop out then, and it still does.

Could it be that some of us enjoy our gender stereotypes? Perhaps so, especially when our physiological differences offer a good excuse for avoiding something.

God definitely created man and woman different. As we stated in Chapter 1, God loves diversity, and we'd be blind if we couldn't see the differences between the sexes. God "created man in His own image; ...Male and female He created them." (Genesis 1:27) And then He gave each a specific role in the world. And yet, the Apostle Paul writes, "There is no longer Jew or Gentile, slave or free, male and female. For you are all one in Christ Jesus." (Galatians 3:28 NLT) Is this a contradiction? Not at all.

The statement in Galatians refers to our eternal value in the eyes of God, as well as to our joint calling in Jesus Christ. Despite our *physical* differences, we are *spiritually* equal in the Lord's eyes, and equally responsible to obey His commandments. But in our less than perfect world, we tend to emphasize our social differences, not our spiritual similarities.

Many of us actually tend to identify with gender stereotypes, and often measure our own self-worth by how much we measure up to the secular ideals of men and women. Hence, women believe they must conform to certain standards in their manner and appearance; while guys think in terms of "Real men don't" do *this,* or *that!*

For those of us who follow Christ, our identity, self-worth, and moral obligations are not based on gender stereotypes or any other social distinctions. The only thing that defines who we truly are is our relationship with the Lord. And as joint heirs in Christ, we have inherited joint responsibility in all things related to God's Word. When it comes to His Biblical commands, we're not free to pick and choose. We can't point to secular stereotypes to justify ducking certain obligations—such as the practice of hospitality.

Sigh! Men, can you guess where this is leading?

For decades, men have identified the art of entertaining, with all its frills and *foofoo,* as a female pastime. We have no desire to refute this male perception, because frankly, we don't *care* if men entertain. HOWEVER, we *do* care (because God cares) if they practice hospitality!

Unfortunately, as stated last chapter, people have confused the Biblical practice with the secular art. So, in their confusion, men now view any act of reaching out, welcoming and serving as being women's work! "*Real* men," they've decided, "*don't* entertain"; and hence, thanks to a popular misconception, "Real men don't take part in extending hospitality!"

When the time comes to welcome a new family to the neighborhood, or prepare for a Christmas gathering or a special celebration in honor of the new pastor, men routinely cling to the secular stereotype of what real men do. In other words, they make hollow excuses to get out of obeying God's command to be hospitable! Remember, guys, we're discussing *hospitality* here, not the art of entertaining.

God's not asking you to make a flower arrangement for the table centerpiece. But He does expect you to take an active role in His sacred practice, to seriously take part in the preparations—and to actually initiate acts of hospitality! Going fishing while the womenfolk visit the new neighbors is unacceptable in the eyes of God.

Of course, we can't blame God's men for being confused about hospitality and their role in it. Again, their misconceptions regarding the sacred practice stem from our society's preoccupation with the art of entertaining, and are but a few of the unintended consequences we discussed last chapter. Furthermore, men aren't the only ones confused.

Regarding the art of entertaining, Margaret Visser explains in her book *The Rituals of Dinner*, that once you designate something as an art, you are defining it as a pursuit requiring creative ability, a specific set of skills, and a proper setting in which it can be executed. And, by its very definition as an art, the pursuit will ultimately be left in the hands of the few artists capable of properly executing it.

In other words, once Martha Stewart and her followers convinced the world that entertaining is an art, most people quickly assumed the secular pursuit should be attempted only by those who have mastered the art. This logical conclusion is yet another of the unintended consequences which has driven people away from modern entertaining.

Now, because our culture continues to saddle hospitality with all the baggage of its secular counterpart, it's not just the men who think God's sacred practice is someone else's business. Guys view it as women's work, but at the same time, many women want nothing to do with hospitality—because these ladies view the practice as a task best accomplished ONLY by someone who's mastered the art! Heaven help us all! God's sacred practice is truly paying the price for all the sins of the art of entertaining!

The art is viewed primarily as a feminine pursuit, so most men have opted out. Furthermore, the art requires an advanced level of creativity and skill to meet its sky-high standards, and hence, most women have opted out. So, exactly who's entertaining these days? A very tiny handful of ladies who've "mastered" the art, or who believe they've mastered it.

Okay ... and how many people are extending Biblical Hospitality? Even fewer! Among the handful who've mastered the art, most are omitting the eternal and spiritual aspects of hospitality—as we stated, they're only entertaining. Everyone else, men *and* women, have turned away from the aggravations, excesses, and gender stereotypes of the art, and because they associate the secular art with hospitality, they've also walked away from God's sacred command to be hospitable. *Ouch!*

Which is precisely why making a distinction between modern entertaining and the sacred practice of hospitality is imperative!

Fact: as we discussed in Chapter 4, the angel named Martha had a message that was right for its time—but that was over thirty years ago! Fact: Ms. Stewart is the quintessential hostess; she is without peer; she is a true Jedi master of the art; she's the standard bearer (and rightly deserves the distinction), the Obi Wan Kenobi of modern entertaining; she is (and has been for decades) *the* role model for the secular art, the one to emulate.

Fact: since the "face" of entertaining is that of a woman, and most of the people who pursue the art are women, guys everywhere have gotten the message "Men Need Not Apply!" But even without the benefit of "facial recognition," the sheer artsiness of entertaining has identified the enemy of "real men" everywhere—and the dainty cucumber sandwiches stacked geometrically upon a hand-cut doily (no two of which, like snowflakes, can ever be the same) or the pomegranate and lemon-grass tea solar-brewed and decanted from a pink depression glass carafe, have sent guys running for their lives, fleeing to the sanity of their man caves!

Fact: based on numerous interviews, "real men" don't entertain!

Fact: extending hospitality is not the same as entertaining.

Fact: hospitality is not gender-specific.

Fact: God does not exempt men, real or otherwise, from His sacred practice.

Fact: men cannot use gender stereotypes to avoid extending hospitality.

Guys, forget about entertaining; God has not called you to decorate cakes or carve watermelon boats. His command to you is far simpler than you were initially led to believe: "Show hospitality to one another without grumbling." (1 Peter 4:9 ESV) Got it, guys? *Hm*, well then, let's see now.... How can we state this another way? Umm, *hospitality* ... uh.... No, that's it. We can't state it any better the Word of God.

Whatever Happened to Hospitality?

And yet, one fact remains: men are conspicuously absent from participating in the practice of hospitality, in both secular society *and* our faith communities. Okay, the world at large tends to get caught up in the pursuit of self and getting ahead. But a lack of participation within the Body of Christ is inexcusable, because God's people should know better! They don't, however, because God's sacred approach to love, acceptance, healing and unity remains the most neglected and misunderstood concept in the Western church today!

If you believe we're exaggerating our claim, ponder the following questions:

1. *Have you ever heard anyone anywhere at any time refer to the God of the Bible as a hospitable God? Or that hospitality is the one single practice/quality that defines His heart? Or that He values it as much as prayer and meditation on the Scriptures?*

2. *Have you ever heard a sermon or teaching on the sacred practice of hospitality, fully explaining it as we have, distinguishing it from entertaining, and pointing out that it's one of God's Biblical commands?*

3. *Have you ever attended a conference, seminar or workshop on the importance of hospitality and how best to practice it?*

4. *Have you ever heard a teaching on the qualities of spiritual leadership (for bishops, deacons, pastors, etc.), as outlined in 1 Timothy 3 and Titus 1, that did anything more than simply speed past the requirement to practice hospitality?*

5. *Does your pastor emphasize the importance of hospitality in his words and actions? Does he train his church leaders in the sacred practice? For*

that matter, do your church leaders set the exam-
ple by extending hospitality?

6. *Does your church have a true ministry of hos-*
   pitality? Or does it simply have a social committee,
   or the standard group of greeters and ushers? If
   your church does have a "hospitality minister," is
   it relegated to the women's ministry?

7. *Prior to reading this book, were you aware of the*
   importance of hospitality, or that it's a Biblical
   command? And were you aware of the differences
   between hospitality and modern entertaining?

We wouldn't be surprised if you answered "no" to most of the above questions; saddened, but not surprised.

We've been involved in church ministry for over thirty-two years, and maintained associations with several Christian denominations ranging from Southern Baptist to Catholic, from Methodist to Assemblies of God, from non-denominational to Messianic Jewish worship. We've attended seminars and taken classes on church leadership and discipleship, participated in workshops, and heard messages from countless missionaries, evangelists, presbyters, and visiting pastors. And we've (pardon the pun) religiously tuned in to Christian TV and radio.

We've benefited from the wisdom and insights of some truly great men and women of God, but strangely enough, during all that time, in all these varied venues, we've never heard a single teaching or preaching on the true meaning, purpose and importance of hospitality, a clear Biblical mandate in both the Old and New Testaments, and a concise command for all followers of Christ.

We've asked numerous pastors and priests, missionaries and evangelists, as well as anyone else involved in church ministry and leadership, about the significance of hospitality. The responses are all about the same. When pressed on the issue, they nod and say they get it. That's good, we're glad somebody gets it—because we sure don't! We can't understand how anyone can truly "get" the importance of something but continue to neglect it in both deeds and words!

1 Peter 4:9 plainly admonishes believers to extend hospitality. 1 Timothy 3 lists the practice as a requirement for church leadership and, as we'll discuss in subsequent chapters, numerous references to hospitality in the Bible plainly illustrate that it's the men who are to take the lead in this vital spiritual endeavor. So we're scratching our heads, wondering "Whatever happened to hospitality?"

Perhaps hospitality is just *our* thing, something we're passionate about and are now trying to cram down everybody's throat. After all, the Body of Christ has bigger fish to fry.

Seriously? Let's examine a few verses.

"A bishop then must be blameless, the husband of one wife, vigilant, sober, of good behavior, given to hospitality, apt to teach;" (1 Timothy 3:2 KJB) Wow, tall order: upright, well-behaved and "given to hospitality"! And notice the order of these qualifications: being hospitable is listed before being able to teach! Here's another translation of the same verse: "...An elder must be a man whose life is above reproach. He must be faithful to his wife. He must exercise self-control, live wisely, and have a good reputation. He must enjoy having guests in his home, and he must be able to teach." (NLT)

The Apostle Paul isn't minimizing teaching skills, but he apparently believes a hospitable nature ranks a little higher in the attributes of spiritual leadership. People can teach from "head knowledge," repeating what they've read or heard or seen in others, and still be somewhat effective; because God's truths have great power regardless of who's stating them: "My Word ... will not return to Me empty, without accomplishing what I desire, and without succeeding in the matter for which I sent it." (Isaiah 55:11 NASB)

And yet, deeds always speak louder than words. Someone once said, "People don't care how much you know; they want to know how much you care!" The practice of hospitality allows people to witness how much you care. It sends out a life-changing message of God's love, teaching the true nature of Christ through practical expressions of love, acceptance and sharing. But it's one lesson that cannot be faked. Remember, hospitality is an <u>attitude of the heart</u>, demonstrated by a lifestyle of giving and serving.

"Since an overseer <u>manages God's household</u>, he must be blameless—not overbearing, not quick-tempered.... Rather, he must be hospitable, one who loves what is good...." (Titus 1:6-8 NIV) If we are to manage God's household, then He expects us to be good hosts! Various translations define a good host as "a lover of hospitality" (KJB); "hospitable to strangers" (ISV); and "he must enjoy having guests in his home." (NLT)

The characteristics described in all these translations are those of a loving person, specifically, a person who exhibits Godly love. The traits of Godly love are further expounded in 1 Corinthians 13, and as we briefly discussed in Chapter 3, these traits define the heart of angel. They also are the foundation of Biblical Hospitality.

Surprised by the importance of hospitality or its relative preeminence in the list of qualifications for spiritual leadership? We wonder what's more convicting, the requirement itself, or the fact it's specifically a requirement for men. Interestingly, we've discussed the preceding verses, along with 1 Peter 4:9, with several pastors from different denominations, with priests and nuns, and others who've been involved in church ministry for decades, and we invariably hear something along the lines of what a dear friend once told us.

He's a Presbyter, and holds a PhD. in Theology. And he made a revealing statement: "I've taught on these very scriptures numerous times; I've discussed the various qualities of a spiritual leader ... the husband of one wife ... able to teach ... but I must admit, I've never discussed being hospitable as one of them. But there it is!" Revealing, but *not* uncommon.

So, owing to the confusion caused by the art of entertaining, men have been led to believe hospitality is for women only. And no one in the Body of Christ is setting the record straight by properly teaching the truth about God's sacred command. No wonder men fail to practice hospitality!

Now, add to the collective confusion of both our society and the Western church, the basic idea that entertaining is an art, along with the misconception that hospitality is tied to that art. The result? Since an art is considered a take-it-or-leave-it proposition, not necessary in daily life, and something to be executed only by those who've mastered it, many people wrongly believe that practicing hospitality is *also* a take-it-or-leave-it proposition, and only for those who've mastered it. Folks, now we've lost most of the women as well. "Whatever happened to hospitality?" It was overlooked, misunderstood, and neglected by men *and* women.

Passing the Buck

When decorating a home, there are definite essentials. The walls must be painted, preferably a nice color. Window treatments (*Curtains*, guys, curtains!) must be installed. A soft carpet is also a must: it keeps the noise level down and makes the room feel warmer. How about some art for the walls? A seascape, a farm on a hill, or something swirly and unintelligible? Framed art can be expensive, though. Furthermore, because it's not essential, art is considered the last "layer" when decorating a home. It's simply a nice little extra. You don't want to walk barefoot on a cold floor, or have to turn out the lights in order to undress; you can't get along without carpet and curtains, but you *can* live without art hanging on the walls.

Similarly, you can get along without the art of entertaining: it can be expensive, and it's not essential. But you can't live without the benefits of hospitality in your life. God's practice is not a nice little extra. As previously discussed, it impacts the most important area of our lives, our relationships. Besides, it's not a take-it-or-leave-it proposition. The Bible doesn't state, "Be hospitable if you feel like it. Practice hospitality if you want. Have guests over if you have the extra time and cash. Obey My command if it's something you're good at." Nor does the Word of God state, "Be thou cunning, and passeth the buck!"

God has called all believers, and especially His men, to take personal responsibility for extending hospitality—with no excuses. And yet, whenever a need arises, whenever someone should reach out to a new family or make sure a birthday doesn't go uncelebrated, the "buck" gets passed around, with no one wanting to

take responsibility. The men point to gender stereotypes, and quickly find more "important" business to
attend to, before unloading their spiritual and moral
obligation on the closest women they can find. (But
what business could possibly be more important than
doing God's will?)

In turn, the women announce, "It's not my *thing!*"
And they further pass the buck to other women who
appear to have an interest in hosting, or a talent for the
art of entertaining, the handful of overworked Martha
Stewart-types! This attitude of "don't bother me with
trivialities" might be acceptable in regards to modern entertaining, and even understandable; but extending hospitality is not a trivial matter. Again, it's a sacred practice, a
Biblical command and important spiritual business, and
God is not smiling at how people cleverly avoid it.

When it comes to doing God's will, no one is exempt. Practicing hospitality is like prayer or giving or
serving or ... loving one's neighbor. Men are not only
called to the practice, but are also expected to model it
as spiritual leaders. Women are also called to the
practice, and not just the "Marthas"! The sad truth,
however, is that over the last sixty years or so, a period
during which our society has become increasingly secularized, our communities and faith congregations have
moved further away from many fundamental Biblical
principles.

The Western church has effectively "forgotten" a
few specific truths; while unwittingly embracing certain
culturally-relevant ideas and attitudes. One of the
truths that's been "lost" among believers is that of
hospitality. The Western church no longer teaches this
truth, and most faith communities no longer model the
practice. God's original concept for social interaction
has been "out of sight, out of mind." Hence, believers no

longer hold one another accountable to the practice of this lost truth.

As with all good things spun into existence by the Creator of the Universe, the loss of the truth and practice of hospitality has created a great void in our society. Our relationships have suffered, our families have deteriorated, and our cities are fragmented. But then, as the prophet warned, "[God's] people are destroyed for lack of knowledge." (Hosea 4:6 ESV) We definitely need an infusion of God's sacred practice!

Our communities and places of worship have tried to fill the void with the secular substitute of entertaining, but to no effect. The void remains, greater than ever, except now we're also dealing with the negative consequences of the art!

It's time to fill the void. Time to repair the ravages of time, neglect and misunderstanding. It's time to rediscover God's sacred concept, and recommit ourselves to the spiritual practice of hospitality. We can use it, the world needs it, and God is waiting for it! He's given us a clear Biblical mandate to reach out to others in love, and it's imperative that we heed the call to be hospitable in every area of our lives.

We'll further discuss the actual practice and benefits of hospitality as we continue to peel the onion. But for now, we need commitment. Without commitment, there will *be* no practice! So, please, stop confusing hospitality with modern entertaining; stop minimizing its spiritual importance; stop approaching it as an art; stop making excuses based on irrelevant gender stereotypes; and stop pawning the practice off onto someone else!

Take personal responsibility for God's sacred practice. Roll up your sleeves, and open your heart and your home. Above all, open your *mind* to the truth of hospitality.

Pastors, we implore you to teach this forgotten truth. Model it by reaching out to people, not just in your faith community, but also in the world at large. Take a personal hand in the hospitality of your church; and extend it to all the "angels" God sends your way— and not just inside the four walls of the church, but also in your homes!

Spiritual leaders, at all levels of ministry, become God's hands extended. Embrace the practice. Become messengers of hospitality. Don't pass the buck. Men, don't relinquish your responsibility by relegating the practice to your wives or other women in the church!

Men, set the example! Follow in the footsteps of the great men of the Bible (one of whom we'll discuss in a subsequent chapter) who enthusiastically extended hospitality. Model the practice and teach it to your children, or your spiritual children!

Ladies, hospitality is not an art; you are more than capable of extending love through a listening ear and a simple meal, or a cup of coffee. So don't throw away God's calling by passing the buck to other women who appear more suited to the art. And please, don't limit the practice to the Women's Ministry, or a social committee, or the designated greeters in the church.

Men, make a difference. Touch lives, meet needs, build and nurture relationships. Women, don't get left out. Help to mend hearts, feed the minds, bodies and spirits of the people you encounter. Men—*and* women— God is calling all of us to return to the Biblical practice of hospitality. He makes no distinctions between gender or abilities, or how much time, talent and resources we have at our disposal. When it comes to extending hospitality, we're all equally responsible, and equally capable—men, women and *angels*!

CHAPTER 8:
CLOSE ENCOUNTERS OF THE ANGELIC KIND

There's an oft-used plot device of weekly TV adventure shows, in which the bad guys kidnap the hero and replace him with a lookalike. The evil double manages to fool most of the people he meets, but those closest to the show's hero, who know him best, eventually realize they're being duped. Life is usually nothing like television, and yet, our crazy world has a peculiar way of imitating, perhaps unintentionally, all the wonderful concepts and principles originally established by God—only with a secular spin. And sometimes the secular "doubles" even manage to supplant the real McCoy!

One day the art of entertaining, looking a bit like our hero, hospitality, crept into the Western church and fooled just about everyone! Who did this secular double look like? Martha Stewart, of course. As we've stated, this multitalented lady is the "face" of modern entertaining. But her "resemblance" to the Biblical model goes only so far.

Then, who's the *real* face of God's sacred practice? Sorry, Martha, but the "hero of hospitality" was born a few millennia before you wrote your first book or made your first TV appearance. And *he's* a ... well, a "he"!

As recorded in the Book of Genesis, the great Patriarch Abraham was the first person to extend hospitality, and his unexpected guests were three strangers who'd traveled quite a distance—all the way from Heaven! Yes, Father Abraham opened his home to three strangers who turned out to be angels. (Honest-to-goodness, supernatural beings from the celestial realm!) We suspect Martha has entertained an impressive list of big-name celebrities, but not even she can top Abraham's guest list!

To the twenty-first century mind, the idea of opening one's door to three strangers sounds altogether alien—especially three strangers who turn out not to human! In fact, the patriarch's singular act of hospitality sounds more like an episode from Rod Serling's *The Twilight Zone.* But then, the sacred practice actually originated from what we can describe as God's "twilight zone"—another dimension we call the spirit realm!

God used (and continues to use) Abraham's interdimensional adventure with the angels to illustrate an important truth about the practice of hospitality. Although the art of entertaining is an earthbound pursuit, extending hospitality is a spiritual endeavor (expressed in a physical context). It addresses not just our physical and temporal needs, but also reaches beyond the here and now, to impact the unseen eternal and spiritual matters of the heart. And its motivating force flows straight from the Creator of the Universe; and it's the strongest force on the planet: LOVE! Moreover, when you practice hospitality you're reaching out to "angels" (God's messengers) from all walks of life! So, may the force be with you!

Even apart from his breaking bread with beings from another realm, Father Abraham is a remarkable (yet flawed) pioneer in the things of God. His character and his enthusiasm for hospitality were our inspiration for an entire series of books examining various facets of God's sacred practice. Like Martha Stewart, Abraham was a multi-talented individual; but unlike Martha, who's mastered the material art of entertaining, the patriarch's talents were more of a spiritual natural. We'd love to elaborate (at great length) on our hero Abraham, but for this present volume, we'll confine ourselves to a few essential facets of his character.

Abraham is the first recorded worshipper of the one true God (Elohim). He existed before Moses, the Torah, the Prophets, King David and the Temple in Jerusalem. His life story is recorded in the first book of the Bible (Genesis 12-25); and the history of his heirs unfolds throughout the remainder of the Bible.

Abraham was initially just another pagan from the land of Ur (Mesopotamia), but based on a double-sided act of hospitality, God chose him to reveal His plan of salvation and blessing for all mankind. The hospitable God of the Bible first reached out to Abraham with an invitation to join Him in a close personal relationship. Abraham, who to this day is known as "the friend of God" (James 2:29), gladly accepted His master's hospitality; but in doing so, Abraham also was extending hospitality to God, by inviting Him into his own life.

Abraham's intimate relationship with his God, along with his legendary act of extending hospitality to three angels, distinguishes the patriarch as *the* Biblical representative of the sacred practice. That God chose Abraham for such an important role is only fitting: after all, God desires each of us to be like Him in our attitudes and actions; and, because He's a hospitable God, and deems hospitality of utmost importance, He chose the most hospitable man among all His created beings—a man with the heart of an angel!

God appeared to Abraham to deliver a promise: "...I will make you a great nation, and I will bless you, and make your name great; And so you shall be a blessing; ...And in you all the families of the earth will be blessed." (Genesis 12:2-3 NASB) So, clearly this man with a heart of hospitality is to have a pivotal role in God's dealings with humanity!

How would God fulfill His promise to Abraham? In the long run, Jesus Christ, the Savior of the World, would come through the Patriarch's lineage. For the time being, however, this was an awfully BIG promise, because Abraham didn't have any kids! And his prospects for starting a family were pretty limited. In fact, when God first promised His friend an heir, Abraham was seventy-five years old, and his wife Sarah was sixty-six and barren! Abraham was a man of great faith, but we can imagine him folding his arms and muttering, "This I *gotta* see!"

At this point in Biblical history, people had longer lifespans. Still, Abraham and Sarah were no Spring chickens. They weren't even *Fall* chickens! And both questioned God regarding the ... *uh* ... logistics of the affair. So God eventually elaborated with these specifics: "...Sarah, your wife, will give birth to a son for you. You will name him Isaac, and I will confirm my covenant with him and his descendants as an everlasting covenant." (Genesis 17:19 NLT) Isaac is henceforth described as the "Son of Promise."

Abraham never stopped waiting for God to fulfill His promise—even though twenty-four painfully long years passed. Abraham turned 99, and Sarah 90! (Can you imagine waiting a quarter-century for a promise to be fulfilled?) But finally, just when the Patriarch's faith in his friend God had been stretched nearly to its limits, something wonderful happened, one of those inspiring "suddenly" moments Lakewood Pastor Joel Osteen loves to share.

Strange Visitors from Another World

One seemingly ordinary day, three strangers showed up at the door to Abraham's tent. There was nothing remarkable about this trio of men. They simply appeared to be dusty travelers on a long journey. Abraham didn't know where they came from or where they were bound. But he realized these strangers could benefit from his hospitality. Little could the Patriarch know, his guests were from the supernatural realm! (Cue the *Twilight Zone* music!)

Three angels in human form had journeyed from Heaven to deliver a message from Abraham's friend, God! And this message was so significant, it would ultimately impact the entire human race. Good thing Abraham hadn't turned these strangers from his door! What was their message? Do you really want to know? Are you sure? Well....

Hey, *chill out!* Abraham waited 24 years. We're sure you can hold out another minute. *Okay!* These Heavenly Messengers announced: "[The Lord] will return to you about this time next year, and your wife, Sarah, will have a son!" (Genesis 18:10 NLT) These angels essentially encouraged Abraham to stay in faith regarding the promise, to hang in there just a little while longer, because the time of fulfillment was near!

The following year, Isaac, the Son of Promise was born. His name translates "he laughs," and it signifies the joy Abraham and Sarah felt at the child's birth! The descendants of Isaac would comprise the twelve tribes of Israel, including the tribe of Judah—from which the Messiah, Yeshua (or Christ Jesus) would eventually come to save the world. So, in fulfilling His promise to His friend Abraham, by granting him a son, the Great Patriarch of the Jewish people (and, through faith, the rest of humankind) became a blessing to *all* people for *all* time.

Of course, things could have gone quite differently; Abraham could have missed out on the blessing completely. In fact, had the Patriarch's heart not been in right place, the Messiah might never have born. Then where would the rest of us be?

Had Abraham failed to open his home to God's Heavenly Messengers, he might never have received what these travelers wished to share with him. Had he not extended hospitality to these strangers, Abraham might have changed the entire course of human history, altering the fate of billions!

Sounds dramatic? Nevertheless, we can't over-emphasize the importance of Abraham's singular act of hospitality! As the spiritual leader of his household, he took personal responsibility for the sacred practice. He could have been too busy with "more important" matters, or too wrapped up in his own affairs. He could have said, "It's women's work," and gone to take a nap. He could have totally ignored his divine duties. But instead, he initiated the whole shebang! He then quickly included his wife Sarah, by asking her to bake cakes of grain. In this way, Abraham's entire house took part in the sacred practice of reaching out to others! (You can read the entire account in Genesis 18.)

Did Abraham realize the significance of what he was doing at the time? Not initially, only that he was caring for the needs of three travelers. He had no idea the men were really angels in disguise, or that his willingness to be God's hands extended would mark a turning point in human history; that his hospitality would open the door to his greatest blessing!

After thousands of years we're still discussing the Patriarch Abraham. We continue to refer to the Creator of the Universe as the God of Abraham, Isaac and Israel, long after our Lord descended to earth in the form of a Jewish Rabbi, the Savior Jesus Christ (John 1:1-5, 14).

Abraham has a hallowed place in the Faith Hall of Fame (Hebrews 11:8); his name means "Father of many nations, or multitudes" (Genesis 11:26); he's the first person to be called a Hebrew (Genesis 14:13); but he's also the spiritual father of Christians everywhere. But we remember him today solely because he had the heart of an angel; because he extended hospitality to three strangers who turned out to be Heavenly Messengers, celestial beings sent by God Himself! We remember Abraham because his attitude of love, expressed through a lifestyle of giving and serving, impacted the world, and gave us the definitive example of hospitality!

Nothing demonstrates the importance of hospitality more than this wonderful event, one of the single most important moments in the history of creation, when Abraham extended "hospitality to angels without knowing it." (Hebrews 13:2 NIV) For this reason, dear reader, Abraham earns the distinction of being *the* Biblical icon of God's sacred practice! And, as a consequence of the Patriarch's hospitable act, God fulfilled His promise to Abraham, effectively birthing the Nation of Israel—and through the Nation of Israel, God ultimately blessed all the peoples of the earth! All because His friend Abraham opened his home to three strangers!

Abraham made sure the angels didn't pass him by! He opened his heart and did his best to bless them. But while partaking of the Patriarch's hospitality, these heaven-sent messengers imparted to their humble host a blessing from God: the covenant blessing that would culminate in the birth of a Jewish carpenter named Jesus—who would take upon His shoulders the sins of the world, and redeem all who receive Him as Savior!

Furthermore, it's no coincidence God places Abraham's historic act of hospitality in the first book of the Bible, or devotes 13 chapters to the man's hospitable life. The Apostle Paul writes, "All Scripture is inspired by God and is useful to teach us what is true...." (2 Timothy 3:16 NLT) What's true (and abundantly evident) in our recounting of this turning point in Abraham's life, is how important hospitality is to God, how impacting a simple act of kindness can be, and how critical it is that all God's people—but especially men, and especially spiritual leaders at all levels—return to the sacred practice as mandated in the Word of God!

Now, before anyone imagines we've taken an isolated incident from the Bible and used it to bolster our claims, we'll point out that the Scriptures are filled with earth shattering events and turning points in the lives of the saints; and just about all of these relate in one way or another to the practice of hospitality! (We'll discuss a couple more in subsequent chapters, but the Bible is so rich in the subject of hospitality we'll save some of other Biblical heroes and aspects of the sacred practice in forthcoming volumes in the "Angel" series of books.)

But Abraham stands out as *the* role model, the *face* of Biblical Hospitality! He's also known as the Father of Faith, and as we'll demonstrate, there's a connection between FAITH and the practice of HOSPITALITY.

We could write volumes on the Patriarch's exemplary faith, but a few words should suffice: Abraham's faith was *enduring!* It was tested for over a quarter of a century, and it never faltered. Abraham sets the perfect example of "waiting upon the Lord"! (Genesis 18; 21:1-8 and Isaiah 40:31)

Abraham's faith had *no limits!* A few years after Isaac was born—the center of all the Patriarch's hopes and dreams, as well as the fulfillment of a promise twenty-five years in the making—God asked Abraham to give up his son through ritualistic sacrifice. None of this made sense: God had never before asked for a human sacrifice; plus He said He'd bless the world through Isaac!

But Abraham was ready to carry out God's will, confident that the Lord had good reason, and that in the end He would somehow provide.... That's faith! And, of course, the Lord was again testing this faith. God provided a far more suitable sacrifice, and for years to come, Abraham and Isaac had quite the tale to tell!

Abraham's exemplary faith is also mentioned in Romans (4:1-4, 9-24), James (3:21-24) and Hebrews (11:8-12, 17-19), in which his life is recorded in the Faith Hall of Fame! But what's this got to do with hospitality?

The Faith Factor

Glad you asked! Reaching out to people takes faith! In order to trust both ourselves and others, it greatly helps if we trust God. The prophet Habakkuk writes, "...The just shall live by [their] faith." (Habakkuk 2:4 KJB) Faith in God gives us confidence that He will guide and bless all our endeavors, including the practice of hospitality.

It takes faith to "love thy neighbor," rather than simply avoiding any unnecessary (and possibly unpleasant) interaction. It also takes faith to share what we have, instead of cautiously hoarding it all to ourselves. It takes faith to believe in tough economic times, God will be our provider (Jehovah-Jireh), and He will multiple our resources for practicing hospitality, and stretch our budget so we can include guests at the table. (The Lord also provides ideas for reaching out in simple but effective ways. Remember our story about the wonders of Spam?)

It takes faith to open your heart and home to others. Doing so makes us vulnerable. After all, people can be unpredictable. Although most of your guests will be "angelic" in nature, gracious and appreciative, it's inevitable that sooner or later you'll host guests who are neither appreciative nor gracious. Often, someone will enter your home when they're not at their best, due to something they're going through; and occasionally you get someone with a chip on their shoulder, sometimes because of their upbringing or background. It's at times like these that the hospitable host has to walk in that 1 Corinthians 13 love we discussed earlier, because true love is *patient*. And, yep, that too takes faith.

It takes faith to heed the message of Hebrews 13:1-2, which states "Keep on loving one another as brothers and sisters. Do not forget to show hospitality to strangers, for by so doing some people have shown hospitality to angels without knowing it." (Hebrews 13:1-2 NIV) This scripture is actually referencing back to the Father of Faith, Abraham, and to his supernatural encounter with God's three Heavenly Messengers.

In certain translations, the wording of Hebrews 13:2 is "some have *entertained* angels without knowing it." This does not contradict what we stated earlier: hospitality is NOT the same thing as entertaining. Nor is the writer of Hebrews stating that "some have impressed angels with their gourmet finger foods and over-the-top tablescapes." As we all know, words have a way of changing over time, and *entertain* is no different. No, we're not *dopes*, nor do we take *dope*. Give us a chance to explain, and we can *dope* things out. Okay? Okay. Here's the *dope* on the word *entertain*.

Centuries ago, the word was interchangeable with hospitality; in its original sense, entertaining included the spiritual component that's been lost in *modern* entertaining. In Fact, in his "secular" textbook *American Dictionary of the English Language*, published in 1828, Noah Webster defines *entertain* as "to treat with hospitality." Webster then uses the word in a sentence by quoting Hebrews 13:2! Wow, how times have changed—along with word meanings.

Over the last few decades, the idea of *entertaining* has taken on excess baggage, such as the aforementioned art of entertaining which has succeeded in driving a lot people away. To make room for this unnecessary baggage, modern entertaining has jettisoned its spiritual aspects; and more often than not, modern entertaining has lost its context of love. It's a sad fact, but people often entertain out of a sense of obligation, or to impress, or to curry favor.

The concept of entertaining, as our more Biblically-minded ancestors viewed it, was a spiritual endeavor, motivated by love, that just might end up with the host having a close encounter of the angelic kind. It was "treating [people] with hospitality"! Alas, as with most aspects of Western culture, such as our educational system, entertaining has been secularized! In the same way our society has added shopping to Sundays, while trying to take Christ out of Christmas, it's managed to add an art to entertaining while bleeding away all the love! The result: like something straight out of a TV show about spies and secret agents, a secularized version of entertaining—an evil double—has replaced our hero, hospitality. (No, we're *not* saying that modern entertaining is evil; it's not! We're just making an analogy.)

Those closest to our hero know there's something drastically different about this secular imposter. It's cold and preoccupied; it's not spiritual, and it lacks love! Our mission? Assemble an elite team of special agents (angels, dear reader, *angels*) and rescue Hospitality from the diabolical clutches of misunderstanding and neglect! Uh, sorry, we got carried away. But, as noted, we can recognize the real deal by its love! The Apostle Peter also mentions hospitality in the context of love, writing "Most important of all, continue to show deep love for each other, for love covers a multitude of sins. Cheerfully share your home with those who need a meal or a place to stay." (1 Peter 4:8-9 NLT)

To further explore the love aspect of hospitality, we'll need to peel away another layer of the onion, exposing yet another big difference between modern entertaining and the sacred practice: the secular pursuit of entertaining, along with its art, is limited to one's immediate social circle, that small group of close friends and family, special acquaintances and business associates. The idea of *entertaining* strangers (in the modern sense) doesn't even enter the picture!

In sharp contrast to this secular phony, Biblical Hospitality *always* makes room for the "stranger." It reaches out well beyond close friends and family, to expand social circles and broaden relationships! Now, calm yourself. By "stranger" we don't mean some nameless person loitering in a dark alley! The Lord wants us to be *hospitable*, not stupid! We live in dangerous times, and evil influences pervade our society, so we certainly need to be discerning and exercise appropriate discretion. We also need to ask God for His guidance. Before reaching out to a total stranger, should you ever have occasion to do so, you must FIRST be led by the Lord!

The Uninvited

The "stranger" is anyone who tends to get overlooked or left out. The new family that just moved into the neighborhood; the new coworker who transferred from another department; the single parent who just started attending worship services; or the college-aged singles who get lost in a church's preoccupation with couples activities, are all possible examples of the stranger. Or how about the cashier who rings up your purchase, or the waiter who attends your table? How about all the elderly folks sitting alone in their rooms at the local retirement center? People we often fail to "see" or think about or interact with ... will continue to be as strangers to us, unless we reach out to them.

These overlooked, lost, forgotten, left-out people need the same kindness, attention and friendship we all desire. These strangers can greatly benefit from our love and expressions of hospitality. But let's face facts: most of us tend to be a little on the cliquish side. We police our relationships as though we were operating a club with exclusive membership requirements. We're interested in associating mostly with people who share the same ethnicity or social and economic background. Anyone who's different need not apply, because they won't be allowed to join the clique!

We tend to feel uncomfortable around those who are different. We usually have to work at relating to them, to understanding their unique circumstances and experiences. Some of us may even be intimidated by the "other"; fearing what's different, fearing the unknown, or simply worrying we'll fail to measure up in comparison to those we meet. All of which is silly, of course! We're all unique, but we all share the same weaknesses, moments of awkwardness, and perhaps even the same insecurities. But we need to remember, we have our eternal value in God alone. Most importantly, we need to discover our own unique identity and sense of self-worth in the One who wonderfully and fearfully made each of us in His own image.

God's reassurance to each of us, in the form of a divine antidote to fear of any kind, is this: "God has not given us a spirit of fear and timidity, but of power, <u>love</u>, and self-discipline." (2 Timothy 1:7 NLT) The Apostle John states, "Such <u>love</u> has no fear, because perfect love expels all fear." (1 John 4:18 NLT) Love motivates our acts of hospitality, and love gives us the courage to reach out to those who are different. Love helps to activate our faith in God, ourselves and others.

The Apostle Paul adds, "The only thing that counts is faith expressing itself through love." (Galatians 5:6 NIV) Together, these two saints are explaining that faith is connected to love, and love is never timid! Now, putting it all together: faith and love take risks; and love and faith working together are the essential components in the practice of hospitality! (Another characteristic of hospitality that makes it easy to distinguish it from its secular double, the art of entertaining.)

Inviting new people into our lives is a true act of love, but it takes faith and fearlessness. We risk disappointment, perhaps even hurt feelings. And we get enough of that from simply dealing with those we already know. So, opening our homes to others is a challenge. Your home is your sanctuary—at least, we *hope* it is—the place where you're most relaxed and comfortable. Hence, whenever there's a social gathering in a home, the host or hostess tends to invite only those people with whom they are comfortable: the same old crowd. And the stranger never gets a second thought, let alone an invitation to break bread. And this sad situation grieves God's hospitable heart.

If we're to be like God, each of us must develop a hospitable heart. Such a heart, like that of Father Abraham, is always on the lookout for weary strangers, fellow travelers along the dusty roads of life who can use a little refreshing, or "even a cup of cold water." (Matthew 10:42)

You may not be able to invite a "total stranger" into your home, but you can certainly show one the same courtesies you'd grant a good friend. You can smile, be polite and even share a word of encouragement. You can also pray for these strangers: either with them on the spot, or later when you're alone. The lesson we learn from Abraham's story is not to ignore the stranger, because these overlooked and neglected people need our hospitality as much as anyone! And the idea of including one of these "strangers," someone who's different from you, or just isolated and lonely, is looked upon as an opportunity to meet an angel—celestial or otherwise!

It's an occasion to hear the story of one of these "messengers"; and, as in the account of Abraham, it could be exactly the message we've been waiting to hear, just what we need in order to grow spiritually. Regardless, faith and love should motivate us to shrug off any complacency and to get out of our comfort zones; to get out of the innate tendencies toward exclusivity and selfishness; to become the kind of *inclusive* people God desires.

Love grants us the ability to view others not as inconveniences but as opportunities; not as threats to our status quo but as individuals uniquely created by God, each with something of value to contribute to our lives. These "strangers" may come from vastly different backgrounds and have vastly different experiences from those to which we're accustomed. And yet, we can gain something special from these strangers—not *in spite of* their differences, but rather *because* of them.

In the absence of faith and love, fear always wins out. Whenever that happens, both you and the stranger miss out on the special messages and blessings God wishes to impart. Abraham wasn't about to miss out, and we'd do well to follow his example! His open-heart approach to three strangers, faith and love working heroically through the practice of hospitality, enabled the Patriarch to receive the confirmation of God's promise, impact the world, and make the history books —through a close encounter of the angelic kind!

CHAPTER 9:
ANOTHER
ANGEL NAMED MARTHA

There's an incident in the life of Jesus Christ which leads our Lord to shake His head and lovingly say, "Martha, Martha." It's an amazingly prophetic utterance, because there are *two* incredibly famous ladies associated with "entertaining"—and both go by the name of Martha!

Martha Stewart we've already met: she's a cultural icon for the art of entertaining, and has been widely praised for bringing the world the message "It's still cool to be domestic, to maintain a home and prepare delicious meals, to plan social gatherings and be creative about it." But, as we've discussed in previous chapters, her idea of entertaining tends to be too elaborate, and has unintentionally impacted our society in a negative way. It's a pursuit that's frequently *not* motivated by love, lacks a spiritual component, and never makes room for the stranger.

As a messenger for social interaction, Martha Stewart is an angel in her own right. And when used as a tool for practicing Biblical Hospitality, her art of entertaining can be put to wonderful use. But over the last few decades, the art has become the means to its own end, with many hosts emphasizing the art over the heart—taking the focus off precious people, and instead placing it on such frills as fancy foods and flower arrangements. As a result, modern entertaining has become nothing more than a social nicety.

Ecclesiastes states, "There's nothing new under the sun," and this has never been more true than in the case of "entertaining." In fact, Martha Stewart isn't the first angel of "entertaining." Close to 2,000 years ago, there was another angel named Martha, who also "entertained." We continue to place the word *entertain* in quotes, because as we explained in Chapter 8, the idea of entertaining has taken on a much different meaning in today's culture. The Martha who lived during the time Christ walked the earth, "entertained" in the same way as the Patriarch Abraham; in other words, she actually practiced hospitality.

The first angel named Martha never hosted a popular TV series or wrote a best-selling book. The story of her hospitality, however, *did* make it into a best-selling book, the Bible (the most reprinted and best-selling book of all time)! What did this Martha do that was so astounding? She opened her home to none other than Christ the Savior, and then served Him a meal prepared with great love! One might expect this angel of hospitality to be praised and revered just as Martha Stewart is. Instead, she's criticized and often maligned! Why? And by whom? To learn the answers, let's journey back in time to the ancient Land of Israel....

THE TIME: 27 A.D.
THE PLACE: SOMEWHERE ALONG A DUSTY ROAD IN JUDAEA OUTSIDE A TOWN CALLED BETHANY.

> *As Jesus and the disciples continued on their way to Jerusalem, they came to a certain village where a woman named Martha welcomed Him into her home. Her sister, Mary, sat at the Lord's feet, listening to what he taught. But Martha was distracted by the big dinner she was preparing.* (Luke 10:38-40 NLT) *She came to Him and asked, "Lord, don't you care that my sister has left me to do the work by myself? Tell her to help me!"* —Luke 10:40 NIV

Martha is clearly flustered by all her preparations, so much that she's gotten upset with her sister—and now, she's committed a double *faux pas!* Not only has she put her guest on the spot, dragging Him into a family squabble, but she's also questioned her Lord's compassion and sense of fairness. Of course Christ cares! The Lord is the embodiment of compassion and sensitivity, and He's *always* caring! But this is a prime example of how flawed people (that's all of us) tend to react under stress. We get emotional, perhaps even snotty, and say stupid stuff (which we usually don't even mean). And Martha is no different. But Jesus doesn't hold this slip of good judgment against His host—just as He quickly forgives the blunders all of us make each day. He *is*, after all, the personification of love, and love is patient and forgiving. (1 Corinthians 13:4-5)

Too bad Bible scholars aren't always as forgiving. Poor Martha made one little mistake, and that's what she's remembered for! Okay, so she let off a little steam, but she did so in the midst of showing her love through a mega act of hospitality! She was indeed an excellent hostess! How do we know? She welcomed a "stranger" into her house, a traveling rabbi—who turned out to be the Savior of the world! (Martha's ancestor Father Abraham would be proud of her!)

Martha was used to opening not only her home, but also her heart. For this servant, hospitality is a lifestyle, and her love includes both the stranger and her own family. Luke 10:38-40 provides an important clue: Jesus is invited to dinner at *Martha's* house. But note, her sister Mary is on hand—because she lives with Martha. Furthermore, in John 12:1, we learn that her brother Lazarus also enjoys her hospitality. (Yes, the same Lazarus whom Jesus later resurrects from the grave!) Which begs the question, why does Luke 10:38 state that it's *Martha* who welcomed Jesus?

If there's a man about the house, why isn't *he* initiating the sacred practice (and duty) of hospitality. (Father Abraham would be disappointed.) And where was Martha's sister, Mary? She didn't take responsibility for the practice, either! (We're beginning to see poor Martha's point in all this.)

By the way, the word *welcome* speaks volumes: it is *well* that you've *come* to my home; as in, your arrival is pleasing, and it has brought gladness. *Welcome* means "a kind reception of a guest or newcomer; to salute a newcomer with kindness; to receive hospitably, graciously, cheerfully and with kindness." (Noah Webster's 1828 *American Dictionary of the English Language*) Wow, the word *kind* kinda shows up a lot! It's a quality that perfectly describes Martha!

No doubt this is why Jesus loved to visit Martha's house. Her home was one of His favorite places, and whenever He was in Bethany, the Lord always made a point to stop in for a little rest and refreshing. Clearly

Martha's hospitality stood out: after ministering to the multitudes, Jesus knew He had a loving, welcoming and comfortable place to relax and visit with good friends; a place where He felt ... at home! What a legacy Martha left! So before we cast stones at poor Martha, we should ponder this: if we were having the Queen of England over for dinner, wouldn't we fuss? Wouldn't we try our best to prepare a meal fit for royalty? That's how Martha felt. She was, after all, about to serve the King of Kings and the Lord of Lords!

Think about someone you'd be honored to host—a visiting missionary, a famous celebrity, the pastor of your church (*hello*)—and imagine to what lengths you might go in order to make that person feel welcome. Perhaps you'd spend all day in the kitchen, or even hire a caterer or one of those Martha Stewart-type event planners. Like most of us, you'd probably fuss! But that's okay!

It's not a sin to fuss a little (key word: "little") over your guests. Even in the practice of hospitality, for which the art of entertaining and "perfection" are never requirements, we should still make an extra effort to give our guests the best we have to offer, to create an inviting and welcoming environment where people feel special and loved. As a matter of fact, in hospitality any and *all* preparations are made with this one goal in mind: to make guests feel loved and special. (And also to make God, the invisible guest, feel welcome! Remember the "Unto Him Principal" discussed in Chapter 3.)

Martha (uh, the sister of Mary and Lazarus; and not Ms. Stewart) knew that Rabbi Yeshua was indeed *very* special! He performed miracles, and spent all His time sharing with others; and *everyone*—"the folks," at least, (to borrow an expression from Bill O'Reilly) were proclaiming Jesus as the promised Messiah foretold by the Prophets of Israel. And even if Martha couldn't wrap her head around this truth, she nevertheless sensed in her heart that this wandering teacher was an important person. So, forgive her, she fussed!

We're certain, however, that Martha's heart was in the right place: she had a lifestyle of hospitality, and hence, the heart of an angel! Her motives were pure and noble, because all she wanted to do was to honor her distinguished guest. She just got a bit carried away. But who can blame her?

An Angel of Understanding

Jesus could clearly see that His host's heart was in the right place. He felt welcomed and loved and special. In addition, He undoubtedly understood her desire to have everything just right for His visit. So He's not chastising her when He says, "Martha, Martha, you are anxious and troubled about many things...." (Luke 10:41 ESV) Although many do believe Jesus is scolding Martha, we have a different take on the matter.

If Jesus were actually reprimanding His loving host, whose only "sin" is being overzealous in her hospitality, and overworked with her careful preparations, thanks to her sister Mary, then Jesus would appear to be unappreciative of the abundant love and care Martha heaps upon her Lord. But we doubt that, because it's Martha's "fussing" and graciousness which has made her home a haven and one of Jesus' favorite stopovers. Perhaps He's just ungrateful, or insensitive and uncaring. Impossible! Jesus Christ had none of the traits of "flawed humans" So what's He really telling His host?

In the Bible, whenever God repeats a person's name, His intention is either to show that the person is very dear to Him, or to get the person's *undivided* attention; or to signal that He's about to state something important. We see two examples of this: when God (in the form of a burning bush) calls Moses, in Exodus 3:4; and when He encounters Saul on the road to Damascus, in Acts 9:4. When Jesus says, "Martha, Martha...." He's signifying His desire to have the *undivided* attention of His busy-bee hostess—who is dear to Him—because He wants to tell her an important truth.

Given Martha's hospitality, it's not difficult to imagine that Jesus truly felt a part of her family. And, although God "so loved the world," and Jesus gave up His life for it (in the ultimate act of love), the Apostle John felt it necessary to emphasize that "Jesus loved Martha and her sister and Lazarus." (John 11:5 NIV) That's a special distinction! So we have sufficient reason to believe Jesus is speaking to His host in the same manner we'd use to advise a beloved family member with whom we're especially concerned.

Jesus is particularly concerned about Martha, because He realizes that while practicing hospitality, she's allowed herself to get stressed out.

During His earthbound ministry, Jesus repeatedly advised His followers NOT to get stressed out over the things of life: "...Don't worry about these things, saying, 'What will we eat? What will we drink? What will we wear?'" (Matthew 6:31 NLT) Truth is, the Lord desires that *each* of us be at peace in all matters, which makes perfect sense: He is, after all, Jehovah-Shalom and the Prince of Peace! So Jesus lovingly advises us, "Don't let your hearts be troubled.... I am leaving you with a gift— peace of mind and heart. And the peace I give is a gift the world cannot give. So don't be troubled or afraid." (John 14:1 and 27 NLT)

Jesus is similarly advising His hostess, when He says, "Martha, Martha, you are worried and upset about many things. But only one thing is necessary." (Luke 10:41-42 Berean SB) He is in essence saying:

My dear Martha, I really appreciate your hospitality, and all the hard work that went into these special preparations. I feel truly honored. And I understand your motivation: by "fussing" over Me, you've made Me feel special and welcome in your home! I also see your servant's heart, and I'm grateful for all you do. But, please relax a little, I'm not a demanding guest. A simple meal would have been fine, especially when served in the loving atmosphere of your home. And, really—although you're an excellent cook and I love dining with you—I didn't come here for the food; more than anything else, I'm here for YOU. I want above all things to enjoy your company.

We can imagine that Jesus is grieved by Martha's stress. He doubtless had intended His visit to be a pleasant and relaxing time of fellowship and sharing for all involved, not an occasion for anxiety and family division. However, it's Jesus' love for Martha, and not disapproval, which prompts Him to warn her about the pitfalls of being *too* zealous in her service.

We can all benefit from the Lord's advice: when opening our homes to guests, we must remember that the practice of hospitality is a simpler, less demanding approach to social interaction than the art of entertaining. It's also less expensive and time consuming than its secular counterpart. God designed His sacred practice to provide an edifying and spiritually-refreshing experience for both the host and guests—who arrive as "angelic" messengers to bless, *not* to stress!

In Martha's case, Jesus turns the situation around, by actually using her stress as an opportunity to share His unique and vital message—which will indeed bless His hostess. (Stay tuned!)

Jesus understood Martha; He realized she had the heart of a servant (and an angel). Surely He was also familiar with the inherent weaknesses of the servant's heart. After all, Jesus Himself came to our world in "the form of a servant." (Philippians 4:7 ESV) Hence, He realized that servants have a tendency to take on too many responsibilities, and to work too hard. In their desire to take care of others and help meet their needs, servants often forget to take care of themselves. Eventually, they can get off balance!

Servants are usually extremely energetic and talented individuals who quickly take charge in order to get the job done. They are doers, fixers, and problem-solvers, making it easy to step back and watch them, *literally*, go to work! And that's precisely what many people do! In the end, they start depending on any servants who happen to be around; and instead of rolling up their own sleeves and pitching in, most people simply continue to lean on these capable but over-worked individuals. It may never even occur to those being "served" that these servants might actually need some help!

Perhaps Mary didn't realize Martha needed a helping hand. But it's far more likely Mary was simply used to having her sister wait on her. If the latter is true, then Martha herself is partly to blame! (We'll discuss Mary and the "one thing" in the next chapter.)

Because servants are usually multitalented, organized, and extremely task-oriented, they can do it all—and often try to! Their strengths can actually become their weaknesses: they are not good at sharing their duties, or asking for help; nor are they good at delegating. Furthermore, because they have big hearts, and are therefore especially generous and loving, they are always going the proverbial extra mile—and they can easily go overboard in their acts of hospitality. Add all these tendencies together, and you get *too* much, *too* often, for *too* many ... which can lead to burn out!

Jesus certainly didn't want His dear friend Martha to get burned out. So, in the hope of helping her restore balance to her life (and her ministry of hospitality), He shared the truth in love, blessing His hostess with an angelic message!

How did Martha get so off balance? First, she tried to do too much. Her preparations got too elaborate—to the point she could no longer handle them by herself. Second, she lost focus of what was most important in the practice of hospitality: she started focusing more on the preparations than on the people she was preparing them for; she started putting more emphasis on the external matters of the meal than on the internal matters of the heart. Food certainly is important, but Martha was spending so much time fixing it that she had no time left to be with her guests!

How many of us can identify with dear, hardworking Martha, whose heart was in the right place, but who lost sight of what's important? Have we allowed ourselves to get stressed out when having guests over —all because we've unintentionally shifted our focus from *people* to elaborate *preparations*, from nurturing relationships to getting all the little details just right?

Have we fallen prey to those unintended consequences we discussed in Chapter 6? Have we gotten off balance, and allowed the art of entertaining, which encourages lavishness, to put a damper on our acts of hospitality? More importantly, will we respond to the truth as Martha did?

And She Loved Happily Ever After!

Let's fast-forward to another visit to Martha's house: "Six days before the Passover, Jesus came to Bethany, where Lazarus lived, whom Jesus had raised from the dead. Here a dinner was given in Jesus' honor. Martha served." (John 12:1-2 NIV) Yes, faithful servant Martha is still doing her thing! But the emphasis of the occasion has shifted. Young's Literal Translation of the passage states that "Martha was ministering." No longer is she preoccupied with "much serving"—her main focus is on Jesus being honored. No longer is she overwhelmed by too many preparations, allowing herself to get stressed out and annoyed with her sister, Mary.

There is once again a peace and calm in the little house in Bethany! Bravo, Martha! She's still doing what she loves and does best, however: cooking and serving! Sure, Martha got caught up in her gifting, but now the proper balance has been restored. We describe her talents and abilities as her "gifting" because Martha clearly has a love and a knack for hospitality. She excels at the practice, and her efforts are both effective and pleasing to none other than the Lord Jesus Christ.

We're all called to practice hospitality, just as we're all called to pray and witness; yet some of us, like Martha, have a special gift for this particular ministry— just as some of us have been called to be prayer warriors or evangelists. None of us are excused from the command to pray, share the Gospel, and be hospitable, but there are individuals, like Abraham and Martha, who've received a special "anointing" (God-given ability) to extend hospitality, as well as a special "grace" (supernatural favor, strength and power) in the practice.

Martha obviously had the "gift"; her hospitality attracted and ministered to countless grateful guests which included friends, family and strangers (one of these being the Savior of the world)! And, despite a few mistakes, God used her gifting to provide a haven of rest and refreshing for His precious Son; *because* "God never changes his mind when he gives gifts or when he calls someone." (Romans 11:29 GOD'S WORD Translation)

In other words, if God has given you a talent for preparing a gourmet meal or creating a beautiful centerpiece for the table, then by all means, He wants you to use these talents in the practice of hospitality. If you've mastered the art of entertaining, He wants you to use it to honor and bless the "angels" He sends your way. Just keep your priorities straight!

We want to be clear on this issue, so, once again: there *is* a "gift of hospitality"; but not having this particular gift (God-given abilities and anointing) does NOT excuse anyone from God's command to practice hospitality. We're all called to be hospitable, and God is faithful to use our efforts regardless of whether or not we possess special abilities. Furthermore, like the "onion" of hospitality, which has many layers, the "gift" can also be "peeled" to reveal different levels.

Although our Catholic brothers and sisters number the gift of hospitality among a list of two dozen *Charisms of the Holy Spirit*, the gift is not specifically labeled as such in the Bible. (A *charism* is an extraordinary ability, such as healing, given to a believer by God's Holy Spirit.) You won't find the gift of hospitality among the "five-fold ministry" gifts (apostles, prophets, evangelists, pastors and teachers); nor is it listed among the spiritual gifts mentioned by Paul in 1 Corinthians

12:28, which adds the gifts of miracles, healing, helps and administration.

The Charism of Hospitality actually derives from two other spiritual gifts: helps, which has to do with service and serving; and administration, which requires organizational and social skills (necessary in both leadership and hospitality). Martha Stewart has these skills in abundance, and has used them in the art of entertaining, as well as in growing and operating the multi-million dollar industry she built around the art. The Martha of the Bible also possessed these skills, and used them to coordinate the preparation and serving of enough food to feed not only Jesus but also His disciples.

We'll discuss how these skills are best used (to facilitate the practice of hospitality) in Chapter 11. For now, we'll simply point out that although the gift of hospitality is not specifically listed in the Bible, the brief scriptural references to the various gifts were not intended to be all inclusive. For instance, a minister of music plays an important role in leading faith congregations in praise and worship, and he or she requires a special musical ability and anointing; and yet, the Apostle Paul makes no mention of the gifting required for this ministry. Nor does he mention the special gifting of people who excel as entrepreneurs, filmmakers, writers, graphic artists, etc.

Paul is not neglecting specialized gifts such as these. He's simply listing key areas, and thereby illustrating that God does indeed bestow different talents and abilities. These *giftings* can be used to bless the Body of Christ and the world, when we offer them back to God through service to Him and the people He created. One way to do this is through the practice of hospitality.

Interestingly, the Apostle Paul discusses all the spiritual gifts (including those necessary to the practice of hospitality) in the context of love. He writes, "...Live a life worthy of the calling you have received. ...Bearing with one another in love." (Ephesians 4:1-2 NIV) The passage serves as a prelude for Paul's introduction of the gifts, a few verses later, which are bestowed to "equip His people for works of service." (Ephesians 4:12 NIV) And again, after discussing the spiritual gifts in his first letter to the church at Corinth, the apostle admonishes us, "...Eagerly desire the greater gifts. And yet I will show you the most excellent way." (1 Corinthians 12:31) That way is LOVE.

Paul follows up his discussion of the gifts with an entire chapter devoted to the subject of love. He essentially writes that without love, all the other gifts lose their power! He ends by stating that even after most of the gifts have served their purpose and are long gone, only "these three remain: faith, hope and love. But the greatest of these is love." (1 Corinthians 13:13 NIV)

Whether the Apostle realized it or not, by establishing the unbreakable connection between the spiritual gifts and love, Paul was also demonstrating the link between the gifts and the practice of hospitality. How so? Operating in the gifts, like the practice of hospitality, begins and ends in love.

- Love is the attitude (and environment) we need to effectively use our gifts for God.

- Hospitality *is* an attitude of love expressed in a practical way. And...

- One of the goals of Hospitality is to create a welcoming (loving) environment.

- The single motivation for any act of hospitality should always be love. Hence...

- Any and all preparations made for an act of hospitality are *solely* to express love.

- Similarly, any special talents (gifts) exercised in the service of hospitality are employed *only* to express love.

The Biblical Martha is the perfect illustration of these connections. She had a gift of hospitality (and a knack for hosting), and she used it, through the practice of hospitality, to make her guests feel loved. Her acts of hospitality were motivated by love; and these acts of love made her gifts and talents far more effective, and gave her efforts a far greater impact!

The Heart of a Servant

Obviously, hospitality requires a little more than love. Love may be the *heart* of hospitality, but serving provides the hands and feet! So, if someone has a special anointing for the practice, it follows that he or she also has the heart of a servant! Martha and Abraham (and all who have the gift of hospitality) were first and foremost servants!

A servant, above all else, serves. This seems like a no-brainer, but a lot people are actually confused about the "office" of a true servant. *To serve* means to wait upon, to minister to, or to render a service which helps meet the needs of life. Martha ministered to her Lord by providing food, fellowship, and a place of rest. A further meaning of the word is "to comply with the commands of" a superior. Any person who routinely performs any of these actions is considered a servant.

A *servant* is one who *serves* the needs and directives of his or her master. For a servant of God, the "master" (the superior to whom we answer) is the Lord; and His directive is to be hospitable, in both our attitudes and actions—by being faithful to practice hospitality. And, as we stated earlier, hospitality itself is about serving:

Hospitality is an attitude of the heart (love) expressed through a lifestyle of giving and serving. The giving aspect of our definition deals with meeting needs, but it's also about giving your time and talents; in essence, the giving of yourself. People who give of themselves do so by making themselves available, by being there! And wouldn't you know it, another definition of *to serve* (as in military duty, whether active or reserve) is being present and involved, or available!

What an incredible multi-layered "onion" we find in the subject of hospitality! We serve God by practicing it, and by practicing it, we're serving others! Similarly, if we're truly God's servants, we do His will, which includes extending hospitality; and in order to extend hospitality, we must become servants!

Those who continually practice hospitality, who have the heart of an "angel," have the heart of a servant, too! Well, actually, the heart of a servant *IS* the heart of an angel! The two ideas are interchangeable!

And while we're on the subject of things that are interchangeable, we'll share two more: *servant* and *leader!* Although one might think the words (along with their meanings) are opposites, God strongly disagrees! Which is why Jesus states, "Those who are the greatest among you should take the lowest rank, and the leader should be like a servant." (Luke 22:26 NLT) In fact, in the Bible the word used to denote an office of spiritual leadership, such as deacon, bishop, or pastor, is the same word used for *servant!* (For some historical background on the idea of leaders as servants, please refer to Acts 6.)

The Apostle Paul was one of the greatest leaders among the first-century followers of Christ. He wrote most of the New Testament, and was the first person to spread the Gospel to the world at large. And yet, the apostle didn't label himself as a leader or writer or evangelist. Instead, he described himself in this way: "Paul, a <u>servant</u> of Christ Jesus." (Romans 1:1 NIV; See also Philippians 1:1 and Titus 1:1) But he wasn't alone in using the word; most of the apostles and leaders who penned books of the Bible (Peter, John, James, and Jude) all call themselves servants. (2 Peter 1:1; Revelation 1:1; James 1:1; and Jude 1:1)

Many of the greatest heroes of the Bible embraced the title of "servant," including Martha and Father Abraham; as well as pastors and priests, deacons and other spiritual leaders, both past and present. Dr. Martin Luther King, Jr. once stated, "Everyone can be great! Because everyone can serve." Indeed, everyone who serves is following the example of our Lord Jesus Christ, who came to earth in "the form of a servant." (Philippians 2:7 ESV)

We discussed Jesus' hospitable lifestyle in Chapter 5. Now, let's discuss another group of servants. The Book of Revelation describes a strange encounter between an apostle and one of their number: "I, John, am the one who heard and saw all these things. And when I heard and saw them, I fell down to worship at the feet of the angel who showed them to me. But he said, 'No, don't worship me. <u>I am a servant of God</u>, just like you and your brothers the prophets, as well as all who obey what is written in this book. Worship only God!'" (Revelation 22:8-9 NLT)

Angels—of the supernatural kind—not only have the distinction of being God's Heavenly Messengers, they are first and foremost His servants! We have a perfect example of this in Matthew Chapter 4: after going through a time of prayer and fasting, Jesus was hungry and fatigued, "...And immediately angels came and began to <u>serve</u> Him." (Matthew 4:2, 11 Holman CSB)

How wonderful! We began our examination of the Heart of an Angel by stating that we are all messengers (primarily, we hope, of God's love), with a story to tell, an experience to share. We are also called to be God's servants. So in a sense, we are all "angels." Furthermore, the angels from the celestial realm minister to God's people, and we in turn are called to minister to others through the sacred practice of hospitality. And now, completing our analogy, we learn that God's supernatural angels and "all who obey" Him (who have the heart of an angel) share the distinction of being servants!

No matter who we are, no matter what our role in society (in our homes, communities, and places of work and worship), <u>we are all called to be servants</u>! Similarly, no matter what talents we possess, whether we have the gift of hospitality, or have mastered the art of entertaining, or simply know where we can grab some good Chinese takeout to share with someone, <u>we are all called to engage in the sacred practice</u>! Whoever we are, wherever we go, God wants us to carry His message of love. He wants us to have the giving and serving, hospitable heart of an angel!

The Biblical Martha had such a heart, which she freely opened to a traveling Rabbi who turned out to be the Savior of the World! Her love and hospitality made her home a welcome retreat when Jesus Christ needed a rest from His burdens, the weight of a world in need!

What an honor to host the King of Kings and the Lord of Lords. What a privilege to create an environment where He was loved and welcomed, a place where He felt totally at home! Martha did just that! If only we could have had such an opportunity! But would we have succeeded in making Him feel special (as Martha ultimately did), or would we neglect Him (as Martha initially did) while being preoccupied with too many things? Could we learn from our past mistakes just as she did?

How would *you* respond if Jesus could visit your home and hang out with you? It's a good thing to ponder, because He *can* visit your home! In truth, whether you know it or not, He already does visit from time to time! And, this may sound shocking but, we host Jesus in our home all the time! We've actually made Him a permanent guest! Not only that, we know others who extend hospitality to Jesus on a regular basis!

No, dear reader, we're not delusional, we're not on drugs, and we don't need to be committed to Bedlam. But we do need for you to trust us on this one, and read the next chapter. All will be explained in due course! Along the way we'll connect with a few more servants from the past and present.

We'll also catch up with Martha's sister, in order to answer such nagging questions as: "Whatever happened to Mary? What did *she* get from her Lord's visit? What exactly was the "one thing" Jesus said she'd chosen? And what did she learn while living in the home of another angel named Martha?

CHAPTER 10:
MY *HEART,*
GOD'S *HOME!*

Martha and Mary's divine encounter with Jesus Christ at their home in Bethany (as recorded in Luke 10:38-44) is an excellent study of two extremes in regards to the sacred practice of hospitality. As we shared in the last chapter, Martha exemplifies the host who tries to do too much. Mary, however, is at the other end of the hospitality spectrum, and represents the person who does far too little. Both of these ladies loved the Lord and wanted to please Him, but each expressed their love and devotion in vastly different ways. Both of these sisters needed some balance restored to their lives.

The Biblical Martha showed her love through her hospitality, which is precisely what God hopes each and every one of us will do. But Martha got a bit carried away with all her preparations. She was a "doer," and she had the heart of a servant. But oftentimes, people who are true servants have a tendency to get carried away with "doing"; and Martha was no different—she got caught up in "much serving."

Although her modern-day counterpart wouldn't popularize the pursuit for a couple of millennia, poor Martha nevertheless stumbled into two of the pitfalls of the art of entertaining! As we previously stated, one of these pitfalls is a preoccupation with overly elaborate meals and preparations, and an inclination toward lavishness—all of which can lead to stress and frustration. The other is the tendency is to focus on these external matters, instead of the people being served. And when the focus shifts from people to preparations, the host loses sight of what's truly important in life, as well as the ultimate aim when extending hospitality: building relationships!

Jesus certainly enjoyed the meal Martha had fussed over, but the main reason He visited her home was to spend some quality time with His host and her family. He desired their fellowship above all things. Anything else that came with it was simply ... icing on the cake!

Martha *almost* missed out on the joy of the Lord's presence in her life. But thanks to a gentle word from Jesus, she quickly learned from her mistake, and as a result, her home became one of Christ's favorite stopovers. And what of Martha, who had the privilege of hosting the Son of God? She earned her special place in the Hospitality Hall of Fame, right next to the Patriarch Abraham. *Good company*, wouldn't you say?

Of course, hosting Jesus Christ isn't quite as unusual as one might think. Promise to keep reading, and we'll explain how YOU too can extend hospitality to the Lord in YOUR home! (Calm down. Take deep breaths.) We'll also share our own experiences doing so, along with those of others; and explain how these experiences tie into the mysterious "one thing" Jesus spoke of! But before we explore these wonderful things, we first need to examine the other extreme in God's sacred practice!

At the other end of the hospitality spectrum, we have Martha's less-than-helpful sister, Mary. Worshipful, she *is*, sitting at the feet of her Lord, taking to heart every word He says—while Martha tries to get some food on the table for their hungry guests. Mary is not concerned, however; she knows how to chill out with the company. But ... *Mary, Mary! You're a little too laid back!*

Thank goodness, Martha was in the house. Otherwise, Jesus probably would have received nothing to eat but a few figs—and He'd probably have to *ask* for those! Mary doubtless wouldn't have thought about anything as practical as serving a meal. She was, after all, entirely focused on the guest of honor. Plus, it's hard to serve in a sitting position.

Mary was so focused on the internal matters of the heart (which is definitely a good thing when practicing hospitality) that she neglected certain *external* matters which needed to be addressed—such as feeding the hungry Rabbi who dropped by for a visit. Definitely *not* a good thing. But then, Mary wasn't the one practicing hospitality in the little house in Bethany. Truth is, Mary was more used to *being* served than to serving others.

Since Martha was such a capable and hospitable servant, Mary had probably fallen into a bad habit: she'd gotten used to just sitting back and letting her sister do it all, including waiting on her and her brother Lazarus. We doubt it even occurred to Mary to give poor Martha a helping hand in the kitchen!

Two sister, two extremes. But the practice of hospitality requires a balance: a little bit of Martha and a little bit of Mary. To achieve this, we need to approach the practice with a K.I.S.S. Mentality: keep it simple, servants! A simple meal is just as filling as seven courses of gourmet cuisine, and preparing it is a lot less stressful, too! And when we're *not* stressed out, we make better hosts. In addition, preparing a simple meal allows more time to focus on the guests (and to connect with them). Remember, "Better is a dinner of herbs where love is, than a fatted ox with hatred." (Proverbs 15:7 King James 2000)

That said, it's nonetheless important to do *something* to make our guests feel special. Providing a simple meal is not an excuse to open a tin of sardines! We want our guests to know we care, so it doesn't hurt to plan ahead and make some preparations for their visit. Like Mary, we want to hear the message of the angels who come calling, and even share our own personal message. But, like Martha, we also need to feed them!

In John 12:1-2, we learn that "Six days before the Passover, Jesus therefore came to Bethany, where Lazarus was, whom Jesus had raised from the dead. So they gave a dinner for Him there. Martha served, and Lazarus was one of those reclining with Him at table." (ESV) Notice that Martha is serving, only this time it's not Mary but rather Lazarus who's relaxing with Jesus. We'll give Lazarus a pass on this one; after all, the poor guy just got back from being dead!

But where is Mary? We can assume that when the scripture states "*they* gave a dinner," the word *they* indicates Martha AND Mary, working in unison. No doubt this explains the relaxed atmosphere, in which Lazarus and Jesus can "recline": not only is Martha no longer stressed out with "much serving," but now she also has a helper! The Word of God further establishes exactly where Mary was, along with what she was doing. Alas, the further adventures of Martha's little sister are for another time. For now, we'll limit ourselves to examining two things Mary got right.

First, Mary found balance. Like Martha, she started out at one of the extreme ends of the hospitality spectrum. And, like Martha, she found her way to the center of the practice. Both sisters expressed their love and devotion to Jesus in their own unique way. Both had the heart of an angel; both left a legacy of love, and hence, made hospitality history. Together, they perfectly illustrate the sacred practice, and we'd do well to follow their examples.

We can easily imagine the Lord smiling and saying to each of these ladies, "Well done good and faithful servant...." (Matthew 25:23 KJB) On the other hand, we can't at all imagine the Lord saying to anyone, "Wow, I was really impressed with your *Pâté de Foie Gras!* You really mastered the art of entertaining!"

The One Thing!

The second *thing* Mary got right was described by Jesus in the face of Martha's initially off-balance approach to hospitality, when the Lord gently proclaimed, "Martha, Martha, you are worried and bothered about so many things; but only <u>one thing</u> is necessary, for Mary has chosen the good part, which shall not be taken away from her." (Luke 10:41-41 NASB)

Like the onion of hospitality, the "one thing" Jesus describes has many layers. We'll peel back each one until we reach the heart of the matter.

- The "one thing" attitude is the polar opposite of the *more-more-more* mentality that rules modern entertaining. Whereas the motto of hospitality is "Keep it simple, servants" (K.I.S.S.), the mantra of the art of entertaining is "Nothing less than the best!" Hence, the art encourages lavishness and having everything *picture-perfect*. It's a demanding approach to social interaction which generally causes stress, unless you're a regular Martha Stewart!

- A lot of "things" can go into the practice of hospitality, such as preparing a meal, setting a table, getting a guest room ready.... The list of "things to do" can get rather extensive. But at the top of every host's list, should be the *one thing* most important in the practice of hospitality: developing relationships. You won't accomplish this (the primary goal of hospitality) if you're preoccupied with too many preparations (as Martha was initially). Remember, people always take priority over preparations in the sacred practice. If you need to sacrifice a few things on your list, it's NOT the people!

  Although hospitality usually requires *some* preparations (the external matters), the focus of any gathering should always be on the people present (and hence, the internal matters of the heart). So, you should never sacrifice spending time with your guests because you're too busy preparing and serving.

Jesus knew His time on earth was nearing an end, for He'd soon be facing the misery and sorrow of crucifixion. He was literally carrying the weight of the world on His shoulders. So He wanted (and needed) the time spent in Martha's home to be an occasion of relaxing and sharing in the company of dear friends.

Similarly, when people come to our homes, we can never fully know what burdens they carry, or what trials they're struggling through. Sure, we may invite these "angels" to share a meal, but we should always be sensitive to their unspoken and hidden needs. Remember, the Apostle Paul admonishes us to "Bear one another's burdens, and so fulfill the law of Christ." (Galatians 6:2 ESV) It's hard to be sensitive to these burdens if we're buzzing about the kitchen like a bee making honey.

We must also remember that "angels" arrive specifically to share their message. Everyone has a story to tell, and sometimes getting that story off their chest can be therapeutic. We need to be present to hear what they have to say; or to encourage them with our own message (of what the Lord has done for us). Sharing a testimony can help restore faith to a weary soul. But again, they probably can't hear us from the kitchen. And we certainly can't give them the attention they need, if we're busy clanging a dozen pot lids!

- Mary revealed the one thing she felt was most important: a meaningful relationship with Her Lord. By sitting at the feet of Christ, she demonstrated she valued His company above all other things. She was hungry for true fellowship with Jesus (her guest). The Greek word for this kind of God-centered fellowship is *koinónia*. From the same term we get the ideas of communication and *communion* (sharing in common).

Koinónia reaches beyond the superficialities of life. It's the kind of fellowship we can't observe with our natural eyes. It's communication that speaks love and devotion without words, because it relies on the language of the heart. If you're married to your soul mate, or have a best friend who's a "kindred spirit," then you'll understand the kind of intimate relationship koinónia produces.

It bears repeating, the ultimate goal of the sacred practice of hospitality is to develop, nurture and strengthen meaningful relationships by fostering this type of koinónia fellowship. The kind of relationships built through the honest communication and sharing of all things, as recorded in the Book of Acts, are what enabled first-century followers of Christ to endure tremendous persecution and eventually flourish.

The Biblical physician, Luke, the only non-Jewish writer of the Bible and the author of one of the four Gospels, described the koinónia of these early believers in this way: "They devoted themselves to the apostles' teaching and to the fellowship, to the breaking of bread and to prayer.... All the believers were together and had everything in common.... With one accord they continued to meet daily in the temple courts and to break bread from house to house, sharing their meals with gladness and sincerity of heart, praising God and enjoying the favor of all the people." (Acts 2:42, 44, 46, 47 Berean Study) Now, *that's* hospitality in action!

- Mary *chose* to sit at the feet of Jesus, and to *hear* His teachings. Being the *Christ* (or Messiah), Jesus had the words of eternal life: as the Prophet Isaiah wrote in regards to the coming of the Messiah: "How beautiful on the mountains are the feet of the Messenger who brings good news, the good news of peace and salvation, the news that the God of Israel reigns!" (Isaiah 52:7 NLT; See also Romans 10:17)

It behooves each of us to sit (be still) and listen to the message of God as recorded in the Bible—with an emphasis on actually *hearing*, and hence, receiving its truths. Oftentimes believers get so busy, they stop listening to God. But, as the Apostle Paul states, "...Faith comes from hearing the message, and the message is heard through the word about Christ." (Romans 10:17 NIV)

We stated earlier that the Patriarch Abraham opened his door to three strangers delivering a message from God. The strangers turned out to be supernatural beings (angels) and their message ultimately brought salvation to the world. Like Abraham, who *believed*, and thus earned the distinction of being the Father of Faith, each of us has the opportunity to open the door to a "stranger" —a supernatural being with a message of Life Eternal. We're referring, of course, to the God of Abraham, Isaac and Israel.

We compare our God to the "stranger" because, for many people, the Creator of the Universe remains distant and unfamiliar. However, if you do perceive Him in this way, it's simply because you've chosen to keep Him a stranger in your life.

But our Heavenly Father is NOT a stranger! He is *not* an aloof, impersonal God. He created us in His own image, in order to establish an intimate relationship with each and every one of us. He is a hospitable God who longs to enjoy true fellowship (koinónia) with us. And (especially for those who already know Him) He wants to have this fellowship *daily!* But He's not presumptuous or pushy: He never barges in, but instead waits to be invited.

Jesus states, "Listen! I stand at the door and knock. If anyone hears My voice and opens the door, I will come in to him and have dinner with him, and he with Me." (Revelation 3:20 Holman CSB) What a beautiful picture of our Hospitable God! He initiates the process of building a relationship with us by gently knocking with His message of Love—gently enough that we must listen carefully. Then He patiently waits for us to respond; but each of us must open the door of our heart.

Like the Patriarch Abraham, we need to invite this "stranger" in. It's the first step to nurturing our relationship with God, and it involves—wouldn't you just know it—*Hospitality!* But we must first open the door of the heart, which is where every act of genuine hospitality originates.

My Heart, God's Home

Jesus said, "Blessed are the pure in heart, for they will see God." (Matthew 5:8 NIV) But exactly how do we "see God" at work in our own personal lives? The Apostle Paul writes, "...Whosoever shall call upon the name of the Lord shall be saved." (Romans 10:13 KJB) Have you called out to Him yet? You needn't yell; He's been by your side all along! You don't even need an icebreaker to start talking to Him. He's actually been expecting you!

But what should you say? The Apostle Paul supplies us with the only introduction we need: "If you declare with your mouth, 'Jesus is Lord,' and believe in your <u>heart</u> that God raised him from the dead, you will be saved." (Romans 10:9 NIV) Like the practice of hospitality, it all starts in your *heart*.

Seems too easy. Right? And yet, it's the "one thing" necessary for salvation, the "one thing" that marks the beginning of beautiful relationship with your Heavenly

Father. Unlike the art of entertaining, which involves a lot of "doing" in the hopes of meeting a set standard, extending hospitality to God by inviting Him into your life requires no elaborate preparations, no fussing, no stress! In fact, Paul writes, "God saved you by his grace when you believed. And you can't take credit for this; it is a gift from God. Salvation is not a reward for the good things we have done, so none of us can boast about it." (Ephesians 2:8-9 NLT)

We can't earn our way into Heaven; we can't work our way in by doing good deeds—not even by obeying the commandment to "Love thy neighbor" through the practice of hospitality. Salvation, along with a personal relationship with God, are freely bestowed, *if* you acknowledge that Christ died on the cross for *your* sins, and hence paid in full the penalty of those sins; thereby satisfying the holiness and justice of God. (We further discuss salvation in Chapter 12.)

Ironic, isn't it? We invite Jesus, but He brings all the goodies!

However, once you do invite Jesus to dwell in your heart, He becomes a permanent resident there. Your heart becomes His home! Writer Robert Boyd Munger draws this excellent analogy in his little booklet *My Heart—Christ's Home.* This thought-provoking resource has been in print for over sixty years, and it continues to remind us of the importance of giving our Lord free access to *every* area of our lives (including the practice of hospitality). Jesus longs to have "the run of the house"; but don't worry. As we observed during His earthly visit to Martha's physical house in Bethany, Jesus is *not* a demanding guest! He only wants to spend a little quality time with you!

The idea of having the Creator of the Universe living within each and every believer is mind boggling!

But it's true! Paul writes, "... Your body is a sanctuary of the Holy Spirit [of God] who is in you.... You do not belong to yourselves...." (1 Corinthians 6:19 ISV) Concerning the last phrase, as we stated earlier, *everything* belongs to God, including you and your heart! After all, He made everything!

But how is this possible? Remember, we have a supernatural God. Jesus said, "I'm sending you what my Father promised. Wait here ... until you receive power from heaven." (Luke 29:49 GOD'S WORD) The Father's promise, as foretold by the Prophets, is God's Holy Spirit! Ezekiel wrote, "And I [the Lord your God] will give you a new heart, and a new spirit I will put within you.... And I will put my Spirit within you, and cause you to walk in my statutes and be careful to obey my rules." (Ezekiel 36:26-27 ESV; See also Ezekiel 18:3, Isaiah 44:3 and Joel 2:28)

The arrival of God's Holy Spirit is recounted in the Book of Acts: "When the day of Pentecost arrived, they were all together in one place. And suddenly there came from heaven a sound like a mighty rushing wind, and it filled the entire house where they were sitting. ...And they were all filled with the Holy Spirit...." (Acts 2:1-3, 4) Note that these early believers were gathered together in a single house; as we previously stated, they were fully committed to the practice of hospitality, and hence, united in koinónia fellowship.

After His death and resurrection, Christ's work on earth was accomplished. He'd sacrificed Himself for our sins, and redeemed us with His shed blood. He then returned to His Heavenly Kingdom and took His place, "seated at the right hand of the power of God." (Luke 22:69 ESV) But to fill His role on earth (and in our lives), Jesus sent the Holy Spirit.

When Jesus took the form of a human and walked the earth, He was limited in that He could never be in two places at once. But the Holy Spirit is not bound by this physical limitation. Not only is the Spirit able to be everywhere at all times, He also takes up residence in the hearts of all believers! Jesus said to His followers, "If you love Me, keep My commands. And I will ask the Father, and He will give you another advocate to help you <u>and be with you forever</u>—the Spirit of truth. The world ... neither sees Him nor knows Him. But you know Him.... <u>I will not leave you as orphans; I will come to you</u>." (John 14:15-18 NIV)

The Holy Spirit is the friend and all-purpose assistant of every believer. The Greek word for Him is *Paraclete*, which essentially means *one who walks with you*. The root of this word reveals the many roles the Holy Spirit plays in our lives: He is the comforter, our advocate, the Spirit who guides into all truths; He encourages, strengthens, and exhorts us; and He intercedes for us! It is ONLY through His divine help that we can live as true followers (disciples) of Christ. And, as with all spiritual matters, only with His help and guidance can we truly and effectively practice Biblical Hospitality.

Furthermore, observe in John 14:15, Jesus makes a connection between love and His sending the Holy Spirit. When you love someone, you open your heart to that person. In the same way, if we love God we'll open our hearts to the Holy Spirit—and make Him feel welcome! Doing so is the ultimate act of hospitality to God (an attitude of love expressed through serving and the giving of oneself)!

Like Martha and Mary, we can have the honor of being able to host (and enjoy koinónia fellowship with) the Living God. In fact, when we choose the "one thing" that's necessary, we can extend hospitality to the Lord every single day of our lives, because He makes His residence in our hearts! And, as with any guest or inhabitant, nothing makes God feel more at home than when we show our sincere love.

Our examination of the "one thing" Mary chose revealed several layers. But we can easily summarize the whole "onion" by describing it as a welcoming, loving, honest, attentive, and responsive relationship with Jesus Christ (the goal of every act of hospitality), after which we give Him the best room in the house: our heart! No, it may not be a "designer home," and *we* may not be adept at the art of entertaining, but it doesn't matter to God. No matter how humble our hearts, as long as they're filled with love, He'll feel right at home! So, open the door to Jesus, extend Him simple, stress-free hospitality, and you'll be able to joyfully proclaim, "*My* heart—God's *home!*"

CHAPTER 11:
HOME is WHERE the HEART IS!

Angels, whether natural or supernatural, have been inspiring people for ages. We've met the two angels named Martha. Now, let's get to know one named Ruth.

When it comes to our own personal practice of hospitality, we're not following in the footsteps of Martha Stewart. We appreciative her achievements, and we realize her popularization of the art of entertaining helped to get people excited about having guests once again. But, truth is, we never viewed her TV specials, books, and magazines as anything more than ... well, entertainment. In retrospect, we're glad we drew our inspiration from a source closer to home: first, because we were able to avoid all those negative consequences of the art, which ultimately resulted in driving folks away from God's sacred plan for social interaction; and second, let's face it, *home is where the heart is!*

Our angel of inspiration never wrote a word on the subject of hospitality, or demonstrated her craftiness on television. But she did plan numerous gatherings and prepared innumerable meals—all with love! And although she's not a media celebrity, she's always been a bright star of wisdom and encouragement for us. And we continue to sing her praises, in both admiration and gratitude, for passing on to us her legacy of giving and serving. So now, without further ado, we present our wonderful role model in the practice of hospitality: Wilma's very own mom, Ruth Lillian Carreras Espaillat!

We'd ask her to take a bow, but she'd just refuse. She's too humble, and too much a servant of God to want to take credit for decades of doing what she loves most—reaching out to others. We affectionately call this kind and unassuming, classy Puerto Rican lady *Mamita!* But then, so do countless others who sense her deep, Godly and maternal love.

Mamita is still serving her Lord at 81. So she predates Martha by a few decades. By the way, that's Martha *Stewart*, not the Martha of the first century! And she has a lot in common with the author of *Entertaining*. For one, Mamita is a multitalented hostess, a regular Susie Homemaker! She was creating "tablescapes" long before they were called that. She was cooking gourmet meals of international cuisine at a time when most Americans didn't even know that French fries weren't French! And in regards to decorating and improvising, Mamita has always thought outside the box!

Her grown children (Joseph David, Wanda and Wilma) fondly remember her flowers, especially her roses, and the fresh veggies from her tiny garden. Apparently, far more than Mamita's thumb was green! She must have had all ten fingers glowing like emeralds, because her garden was an amazing and endless blessing to both friends and family. In fact, her daughters called it the "Magic Garden" (*without* knowing about the kid's TV show, at the time). She'd use her veggies in delicious soups and stews, and arrange her flowers to create explosions of fragrance and color.

Mamita's fresh flower arrangements have been awarded blue ribbons by her garden club; and her arrangements of silk flowers adorn several rooms in our home, which are also decorated with her lovely window treatments. (She's a fabulous seamstress, too!) And yes, we're gushing like an oil well, but it's not crude spewing forth—it's genuine love!

As with many people blessed with the gift of hospitality, Mamita has also mastered the art of entertaining. Hence, her culinary, artistic, and organizational skills have enabled her to extend hospitality with love, grace, and a degree of flair—but minus the stress! Like Martha and Mary of Bethany, Mamita found the right balance in the sacred practice.

We pray that you'll be able to do the same. If you're involved with the art of entertaining, by all means use it in the service of Biblical Hospitality, to help make your guests feel special and welcome. But please avoid the pitfalls of the art: striving to get everything picture-perfect; spending more time, energy and money than you can spare; and stressing out as a result!

Once you realize that nothing will *ever* be PERFECT, and that when motivated by love, your best efforts are not only sufficient but also quite effective, you'll relax and start getting the hang of hospitality. And once you get the hang of it, you'll realize that God's type of social interaction is stress-free and fun! Your guests will feel at ease and right at home—and you'll feel right at home with guests!

There's an expression in the Hispanic culture, which we're certain you've heard: ¡Mi casa es su casa! It means "my house is your house" (as in, *Make yourself at home).* This was certainly the attitude in the Espaillat household when Wilma was growing up.

Wilma's father, David Onelio Espaillat, was born in the Dominican Republic.[3] He met Ruth in "the Big Apple," where they were married and started a family. Their children were born in Manhattan, NY and raised in New Jersey, and all three are as American as apple pie. Yet they greatly benefitted from growing up in a bilingual and bicultural home. Having an anchor in the Hispanic culture added to Wilma's passion for hospitality. For many Latinos, especially those of previous generations, *¡Mi casa es su casa!* expresses both a philosophy and a lifestyle. The sacred practice is an integral part of their culture and identity! So, when someone with a Hispanic background tosses out this seemingly quaint expression, they truly mean it!

Your Serve!

Certain other countries and cultures are strongly linked to the practice of hospitality, as well. Interestingly, the United States was once famous for it. Previous generations of Americans, whether secular or faith-filled, viewed hospitality as an important virtue and essential to the fabric of their country. Alas, times change. Even among the followers of Christ, the practice has fallen by the wayside, the victim of misunderstanding and neglect. Some have tried to replace it with modern entertaining, but the secular pursuit can never fill the void left by Biblical Hospitality.

---

[3] David Onelio Espaillat played a significant role in the history of the Dominican Republic. For additional historical and biographical information please see the Endnotes on page 191.

Modern Entertaining is generally *infrequent*: it's a one-time act or limited series of carefully planned activities held at the convenience of the host. Its execution is often bound by perfectionism, excess, and stress. It's usually practiced during holidays, special occasions, or around an activity such as watching a sporting event on TV.

"Angels" sometimes arrive unannounced, and needs can arise at a moment's notice, but regardless, *entertaining* still requires advance planning, scheduling and preparation in order to meet the high standards of the art!

Biblical Hospitality is a lifestyle, an *ongoing* practice, 24 hours a day/seven days a week, and it's characterized by spontaneous acts of giving and serving—whether it's convenient or not. As such, whenever and wherever a need arises, the heart an angel responds in a practical way. So, extending hospitality involves a degree of *sacrifice*—almost a dirty word in our hedonistic culture!

Wilma learned this first hand from her mom, who was always "ready." Mamita taught her children to love their home and to take care of it; to pitch in and take an active role in hospitality. Hence, their home was always clean and orderly, and the entire family was always prepared for any unexpected guests who might drop by. Things weren't "perfect," but the house was always neat and presentable, and very welcoming.

Having company over never seemed like a big deal. The Espaillat home was always ready for company, and having company was a routine affair. As a matter of fact, hospitality was a breeze, because (to quote another

Spanish saying) *Donde come, uno comes dos* which translates "Where one eats, *two* can eat." Or, to quote an English phrase, "The more the merrier!"

With this idea in mind, Wilma's Mamita and *Papi* (who was also an excellent cook, by the way) always prepared extra food, just in case someone extra showed up at the table—which was usually the case! They knew the extra portions wouldn't go to waste: if no angels dropped by, it was okay, because the leftovers were even tastier the next day!

We've adopted the same approach in our own home today. Make a little more for a friend, or a rainy day—*or a rainy day when a friend in need shows up!* We really want to be ready to feed any unexpected angels at the door. We've even devised an Emergency Hospitality Kit, which allows us to whip up a meal in a few minutes. This can be a real lifesaver, because in all things, including our giving and serving, we always want to "Be prepared, whether the time is favorable or not." (2 Timothy 4:2 NLT)

Serving is an essential part of hospitality. But frankly, serving is hardly ever convenient! People arrive, and needs arise, at the most inopportune times; and plans can change at the drop of a hat. Face it, "life happens"—and it rarely sticks to a carefully planned schedule, or bothers to consult our appointment books! But wherever and whenever a real need arises, be it physical, financial, emotional or spiritual, the hospitable heart of an angel responds in love, even if meeting the need is not simple or easy or convenient.

Dropping by to welcome a new neighbor, or preparing a covered to take to a shut-in may eat into your leisure time. Visiting a sick friend, acquaintance or co-worker in the hospital might take you well out of your way. Making a phone call, mailing a greeting card, or even sending an e-mail to encourage someone may seem like too much trouble. And having guests over for a meal and fellowship may seem like something to be postponed for another occasion. None of these practical expressions of hospitality are convenient, but the loving, generous, serving heart of an angel neither complains nor procrastinates.

We all live busy lives, and not one of us is allotted more than the normal 24 hours a day to get things done. So, even fun stuff such as birthdays, holidays, and other celebrations and special occasions, can come as inconvenient interruptions to our plans. But Godly love motivates us to get out of our comfort zones, to shrug off the natural tendencies to be selfish and self-absorbed, to go the extra mile (Can you say, *Sacrifice?*) —and ultimately to care for and serve others. The Apostle John admonishes us to demonstrate this kind of love in practical ways: "Little children, let us not love in word or talk but in deed and in truth." (1 John 3:18 ESV)

In his book *Improving Your Serve*, Charles Swindoll writes, "Love is never passive." To the contrary, love propels us into action! Again, love is the heart of hospitality—but serving provides its hands and feet!

When a need arises, whether seen or unseen (sensed), the heart of an angel prompts a *true* servant to spring into action, in a sincere attempt to meet that need through a practical expression of love. The Apostle Paul states, "Don't just pretend to love others. Really love them.... Love each other with genuine affection, and take delight in honoring each other. Never be lazy, but work hard and serve the Lord enthusiastically.... When God's people are in need, be ready to help them. Always be eager to practice hospitality." (Romans 12:9-13 NLT)

This is the kind of love and hospitality Wilma and her siblings experienced growing up in the Espaillat home. Their parents continued to serve and honor those around them, in practical ways and regardless of the circumstances or timing. Because for Mamita and Papí, people were never an inconvenience.

Hospitality Begins at Home

We've all heard that "Charity begins at home." Fair enough.

If there's a problem at home, or a family member who has a need, addressing that need or problem should always take priority. We have a sacred responsibility, and are thereby obligated, to care for the needs within our own homes before venturing out into the world to meet the needs of others. This is actually scriptural. (1 Timothy 5:8) Our loving and hospitable Heavenly Father is a God of Order; so He wants us to have a sense of order in our lives, and to keep our priorities straight.

A believer's list of priorities, in order of importance, are as follows:

God: "Jesus [said] 'You must love the LORD your God with all your heart, all your soul, and all your mind. This is the first and greatest commandment.'" (Matthew 22:37-38 NLT)

Your Neighbor: "A second is equally important: 'Love your neighbor as yourself.'" (Matthew 22:39 NLT) The concept of one's neighbors is inclusive of *all* people, but it begins with those *closest* and then gradually spreads outward. The concept follows the same priority for spreading the Gospel: "...Ye shall be witnesses unto me both in Jerusalem, and in all Judaea, and in Samaria, and unto the uttermost part of the earth." (Acts 1:8 KJB)

Obviously those closest to us are our friends and family. Note that Christ says nothing about us taking care of ourselves. Because Jesus knows we'll have no problem doing this without being told! In fact, how we care for our own needs is the gold standard against which we're to measure how much we care for and meet the needs of others: "Love your neighbor as <u>yourself</u>."

In the King James translation, the word *love* is used interchangeably with *charity*. Charity, as we define it today, is any practical or tangible expression of love. But wait a minute! That's the definition of hospitality, too! Yes, hospitality and charity are both "love in action"! *And...*

Hospitality, like charity begins at home. Your home should be the first place you extend hospitality. First, following the order established by the Bible, extend hospitality to God. "Home is where the heart is"—and your heart is where God longs to be invited. Welcome Him into your heart and allow Him the run of the house. He wants to be a part of every area of your life, including the sacred practice of hospitality.

A heart filled with love is what makes God truly feel welcome. Once Christ has made Himself at home in your heart (and life), the love He gives to you (and you to Him) will spill over to others, and fill your house like a warm, comforting aroma; people who enter your home will be able to sense a welcoming atmosphere of love, hope and acceptance—the presence of your hospitable God!

People are what makes a house a home, but L-O-V-E is what makes a house welcoming to people. Sharing this love with your "neighbors" will further reassure God that *He's* welcome in your heart, home, and life. Because, people are created in God's own image and hold a spark of the divine; and God commands us to love *Him* by loving *others*. (Matthew 22:39)

Furthermore, your own family members should be the first to sense this love: the welcoming presence of your Lord, the God of hospitality. After all, hospitality (God's love demonstrated through practical expressions of giving and serving) begins at home! Following God's natural order for life, your spouse, children, parents, etc. should be the frontline recipients of your hospitality. Mind you, this does NOT mean you don't have to extend hospitality to those outside your home. The "reach" of your hospitality first touches your immediate family, but then extends beyond to "Judaea ... Samaria, and unto the uttermost part of the earth." (Acts 1:8 KJV)

No, you don't have to take a welcome basket to your "neighbors" in Timbuktu. But you do need to remember that hospitality always makes room for the stranger—natural or *supernatural*, who carries a message of blessings and greetings.

But fear not, beating within the hospitable heart of an angel is enough love for friends, family *and* strangers; enough love to go around and to empower innumerable acts of kindness. Your spouse, children, and other loved ones should always be the *first* to drink from your well of kindness, but the overflow (the runoff) should be used to refresh those outside your immediate family.

When guests partake of your hospitality, the love and attention they receive, the food you serve, along with any "fussing" you do over them, should be a natural extension of what you daily give your own family. Unfortunately, thanks to today's emphasis on the art of entertaining, many people have gotten their priorities reversed: having company over for dinner has become this stressful struggle to meet the super standards of Martha Stewart and her ilk; to pull off an extravagant and impressive "event"—and who in their right mind wants to go through all that trouble just for the "fam"? Yet another reason why we need to restore balance.

Do you ever prepare or plan a special meal just for your family? Or pull out the nice china just for them? Do you only clean the house or tidy up things when company's coming? Do you put as much love into taking care of your family as you do when "entertaining" guests? Does your family feel as special as you try to make your visitors feel? If not, then what message are you sending these "angels" who live with you?

Hospitality begins at home! Sure, there will be times when your preparations for guests exceed what's routine in your home. But what's routine in your home, the expressions of love you daily show your family, should always be indicative of the hospitable heart of an angel. If not, there's a good possibility your "acts" to promote social interaction are just *that*: acts! Ouch. That might hurt, so going forward, please make sure that's not you.

Wilma fondly remembers her mom's genuine expressions of hospitality when no one else was around but the family. Mamita would frequently plan a special meal and set a pretty table just for the angels in her home. She wanted to show her family the same degree of "fussing love" she showed her guests! Now, obviously, she couldn't fuss every single night, but she did fuss enough over her immediate family that they felt like ... well, honored guests!

Mamita was also careful to keep her home clean and looking nice for her husband and children. And this, along with her other expressions of love to her family, ultimately facilitated her hospitality to others.

Since her house was always ready, and since she'd usually prepared a special meal "just because," it was never a big deal if someone showed up unannounced around dinner time. Mamita would simply set another place at the table for her impromptu guest. But, because everything looked so nice and inviting, her impromptu guest probably wondered if he or she had actually been expected! And in a sense, they *had* been! (Hospitality always makes room for the "stranger"!)

Most times, however, Mamita and Papí wouldn't simply wait for an unexpected visitor; since everything was generally so nice and neat, Wilma's parents would think of someone who needed a little TLC and call them for a spontaneous get-together. They could always think of someone who needed food, fellowship and encouragement, and these "strangers" truly enjoyed being treated like family! So, in creating a welcoming environment for her own family, Mamita's *hospitality at home* spilled over to bless others! That's a win-win scenario!

If you want peace and harmony in your house, if you want a better relationship with your spouse or children, make them the *first* recipients of your hospitality! First, your expressions of giving and serving will strengthen the relationships in your home; and second, you'll be teaching by example what it means to be hospitable (Christlike). Thirdly, your family belongs at the top of God's natural order for life, and keeping them a priority in all things will work wonders—on both a natural and a supernatural level. Try it, and see for yourself!

Of course, if you're already practicing hospitality at home, and thereby enjoying the blessings of a strong family unit, please consider sharing these blessings with others. Share your loving home, hearty meals, and healthy family with people outside the four walls of your "castle." The next time you make your delicious meatloaf or that mac and cheese dish your kids love, why not invite the new couple that just moved into the neighborhood, or that single parent who could really use a break from the kitchen. Next time you're having pizza night, call up a single person, who rarely gets to have pizza (usually because he or she doesn't have kids, and can't eat a whole pie all by themselves).

There's always more than enough love to go around. Start with family, and then let the blessings overflow to your world!

Hospitality is a Family Affair!

Now that the "fam" is rubbing its collective hands in glee, while anticipating getting the royal treatment, we'll throw out one of favorite words once again: BALANCE!

Everybody can benefit from a little TLC, including the chief cook and bottle-washer! Yes, even the resident angel-in-charge needs to be on the receiving end of hospitality every now and then! So, kids, whatcha doing for mom and dad to show your love?

Hey, "Hon"! (You don't mind if we call you *Hon*, do you?) Whatcha doing for your spouse tonight? Please don't forget what the physician Luke wrote: "You should remember the words of the Lord Jesus: 'It is more blessed to give than to receive.'" (Acts 20:35 NLT)

In other words, don't always hang out on the receiving end of hospitality; being on the giving side (the side of the angels) is good for the heart—plus, it gives your "friendly neighborhood servant" a much needed break.

Seriously, the practice of hospitality should be a family affair—with everyone pitching in. Since hospitality begins at home, the whole family (those mature enough, at least) should be involved. And when company is coming, each and every member should be assigned a special task or responsibility to help make the guests feel welcome—before, during, and after the gathering.

Sounds like a fantasy? Well, in a home where hospitality is a lifestyle, everyone will eventually want to get in on the practice! In our own home, we even assign a duty to our pets! Throughout the years, our pooches have been official greeters. (Oh come now, who doesn't melt at the sight of a pooch wagging her tail?)

When we were growing up, we looked forward to having company. Even as children, because we practiced hospitality on a regular basis, we were comfortable with both the practice and our guests. But in helping our parents, we understood that any and all of our preparations were made with one goal in mind: to help visitors to our homes feel welcome. We knew it wasn't about us.

In the sacred practice of hospitality, it's not about who's on stage or who gets credit. It's not about the host or hostess, or their abilities. It's not about the meal, or the decorations, or how well little *Cindy-Lou Who* can play the piano. What's on display is God's love! And love is what you're serving your guests!

Hospitality is a virtue we want to teach our children. It's also a Biblical command and a sacred practice we should share within our homes, in the same way (we hope), that families share in prayer and worship. Hospitality shouldn't be a chore for anyone. It should be a privilege to serve God's "angels"!

And hospitality should be a team-effort. No host should get saddled with the entire responsibility. God has called us all to hospitality—even spouses who'd rather be off fishing!

Wilma's Mamita never got stressed out with "much serving"; nor did she strive to meet the high standards of the art of entertaining, even though she'd mastered the art. To begin with, she was practicing hospitality, not performing like a prize race horse. She wasn't concerned with "being in the winner's circle," she only wanted to make her guests feel welcome, special, and loved. And she was never exhausted by the "mechanics" of hospitality, because she never had to run around doing everything herself. She had assistance from a band of little angels!

Mamita never had a problem asking for a helping hand. Why would she? Her practice of hospitality was not bound by pride: she never felt the need to do it all— and all by herself. She knew it was a family affair!

This team-effort approach to social interaction is in sharp contrast to the art of entertaining. First, entertaining is generally a solo act. It's also viewed primarily as a feminine pursuit. In modern entertaining, the hostess essentially takes center stage. It's her gifts and talents, her home and all the preparations which are on display. It's become a one-woman show, at the end of which, she gets to take a bow for a job well done!

Unless you're Martha Stewart, or someone like her, who's mastered the art, this secular approach to "social interaction" can be very intimidating. And it's ultimately overwhelming to the average person. So, as we stated before, most people don't look forward to "entertaining"! And because they erroneously believe that modern entertaining and hospitality are the same thing, they equally dread God's sacred practice. Trust us, at this sad state of human affairs, all the angels in heaven mourn!

When pursuing the art of entertaining, EVERY-THING, from the gourmet meal to the elegant center-piece to the least and very last "perfect" little detail, falls upon the narrow shoulders of the hostess. That's a huge weight of responsibility to bear, and it's the reason many of these would-be masters of the art start to fall to pieces right around the time the front doorbell rings. And the moment the guests walk through the door they can sense the overwhelming stress and frustration. They can "feel" the heavy atmosphere of turmoil, and perhaps even regret, that greets them! It's not, however, a very welcoming "greeting"!

In contrast to modern entertaining, hospitality is, and always has been, a family affair. It's not a one-woman act in which the hostess must jump through hoops! Everyone does their part, in a relaxed atmos-phere of love and cooperation, and with the expectation of a simple yet enjoyable time of breaking bread and building relationships. When guests arrive, they can immediately sense the peace of God in the house: order, harmony, unity and, above all, abundant and over-flowing hospitality! They feel welcome, at ease, and blessed to be able to share in this refreshing environ-ment. They feel ... *special!*

But it takes a family serving God together, and sharing in all things good and Godly. It takes an approach that ensures hospitality will continue to be a family affair!

When the sacred practice of hospitality begins in the home, it soon becomes a way of life: it starts in the heart, when God is invited in; and then its love flows out to bless everyone in the house. Hospitality manifests itself through practical expressions of giving and serving, but to the family first and foremost.

Through these acts of love, parents model the virtue and lifestyle of hospitality, and their kids eventually follow their lead. Ultimately the children learn the joy of giving and serving, and the value of not being selfish. Spouses learn to cooperate for a greater good; relationships are strengthened, and families become more secure.

Finally, these families share their joy and blessings with others, ministering to those who may be "strangers" to the love of God, or to the love of a *Godly* family. Through the continued practice of hospitality, their homes become havens of rest and refreshing, whether physical, emotional, or spiritual. Within the comfort and welcoming warmth of their own homes, these families serve together, like tiny bands of angels, to fulfill the mandate to "love thy neighbor"! These families have learned that "Home is where the heart is!"

CHAPTER 12:
THE HEART OF AN ANGEL

Are you still with us, dear reader? Please don't abandon us now! We're on the home stretch!

As we stated last chapter, hospitality (like charity) begins in the *home*—and "Home is where the heart is." Actually, we can't take credit for that last nugget of wisdom. The Roman author, naturalist, and philosopher "Pliny the Elder" (AD 23 - August 25, AD 79) said it first. And how right he was! Hospitality begins in the "home" of our hearts, when we welcome Jesus Christ into every area of our lives. Then our hospitality spills over into our *physical* surroundings—first within our homes as we minister to our families, and then to the world beyond.

Here's another nugget of wisdom, from a slightly less distinguished source, but no less true: all the modern-day gurus of interior design frequently state that "the kitchen is the heart of the home"! We agree! In the same way that the human heart nourishes the body with continuous bursts of blood, from the kitchen come frequent meals that sustain the entire household.

Furthermore, when you invite people over, if allowed to roam freely, the kitchen is where your guests tend to gather. People don't want to get left out; no, they want to hang out with you in the "heart of things." And everyone knows, whether your kitchen is big or small, that's where the action is!

Before we go any further, let us reassure you: it's not what's in your kitchen that's important, it's what comes out of your kitchen. A humble heart can supply a whole lot of love! Also, your kitchen doesn't need to be stocked with all the latest gadgets or high-tech appliances to be functional; nor do you need hand-rubbed custom cabinets or those highly coveted countertops of polished granite.

You do, however, need to keep your kitchen clean! Because, first of all, a dirty kitchen isn't very inviting. Would you want to eat in a restaurant famous for keeping a dirty kitchen? Yuck! In fact, restaurant kitchens are periodically inspected by the health department for cleanliness, and if one repeatedly doesn't pass muster, the owner is forced to close until he or she cleans up their act! (Um, literally.)

On a recent Dr. Oz program, experts acknowledged that the kitchen was often the dirtiest room in the house! (Yes, even dirtier than the bathroom!) Even in the "cleanest" kitchens, the ones where the cooks always wash their hands and carefully preserve and prepare their foods, there was ... (cue the creepy music) ... nastiness unseen by the human eye! (Oh, the horror!) When kitchen surfaces were viewed under a microscope, experts discovered germs and bacteria lurking in corners and crevices. And one huge source of bacteria? The always damp sponge used to wash the dishes was a breeding ground for the little buggers!

Now mind you, these kitchens looked and smelled clean; the people maintaining them were careful and conscientious and thought they were doing a good job. But under closer scrutiny their kitchens—the hearts of their homes—had all their dirty little secrets brought to light!

There are a lot of nasty little critters breeding in our hearts. Every one of us needs to take steps daily to keep our hearts sanitized, and hence, healthy. Like our kitchens, we all harbor dirty little secrets, often undetected because we simply don't take time to thoroughly examine our hearts.

Harmful parasites such as wrongful attitudes (prejudice, bigotry, jealousy, envy, strife, selfishness, self-centeredness, pride—*hello!*—and numerous other inhospitable mindsets, so please feel free to fill in the blank) as well as unbelief. Sometimes a slight, whether intentional or not, can lead to a person holding a grudge. If not dealt with, a grudge leads to bitterness, and bitterness is a silent killer of the heart—and the practice of hospitality!

The author of the Book of Hebrews writes, "Work at living in peace with everyone, and work at living a holy life, for those who are not holy will not see the Lord. Look after each other so that none of you fails to receive the grace of God. Watch out that no poisonous root of bitterness grows up to trouble you, corrupting many." (Hebrews 12:14-15 NLT) Part of the *work* involved in keeping our lives holy, and free of poison, bitterness and corruption, is taking the necessary steps toward maintaining a clean heart. Home is where the heart is, so a "messy" heart means a messy home, and—hey, wait a minute!

If you're like us, and can truthfully say "My heart, God's home, then you'll definitely want to keep Jesus' "room" nice and clean. A clean home, like a clean kitchen, is more inviting and demonstrates a greater commitment to hospitality! Have you ever been on a long road trip and were forced to stay in a seedy-looking motel? You know, like the one Norman Bates ran in the movie *Pyscho*—with soiled carpet, discolored sheets and peeling wallpaper? If you're brave enough to take a shower, you need to wear flip-flops just to keep your feet clean! Afterwards, you figure it's safer (and more comforting) to sleep on top of the covers, instead of beneath them!

That's not really inviting, *at all!* Now, pause a moment and contemplate: is your guest of honor, Jesus, hoping you'll eventually get around to cleaning His room? Hospitality begins in the heart—*er*, home! So how does one maintain a clean heart? Let's return to our analogy between the heart and the kitchen (the heart of the home).

Sanitizing a kitchen calls for strong measures such as ammonia and bleach. (*Um*, only not at the same time!) Getting your heart spic and span calls for similar measures. The idiom "spic and span" comes from root words and imagery suggesting fresh, clean wood and the new beams of a sound sailing vessel. Similarly, when our hearts are made <u>new</u> by the work of the Holy Spirit of God dwelling within us, and then kept <u>clean</u> and <u>fresh</u>, the "environment" of our lives is more pleasant to Jesus, and more welcoming to our families, friends, and "strangers."

Clean hearts are healthy and happy hearts, like those of the angels, and more apt to engage in the sacred practice of hospitality. Face it, you wouldn't hesitate to open wide the door to your house when it's clean and neat; but if it's a mess, you might not even answer the door! Well, the same can be said about the heart: when it's clean, you're more likely to open it to others!

King David understood the need to keep his heart spic and span. But he also knew his limitations, so he asked God to do all the emotional and spiritual housework. David prayed, "Have mercy on me, O God, according to your unfailing love.... Wash away all my iniquity and cleanse me from my sin. (Psalm 51:1-2 NIV) Note that David *asks* the Lord to cleanse Him. Israel's greatest King realized that, although it's God who does the actual scrubbing, he had to initiate the cleaning process by being an open and willing vessel.

David must have done a pretty good job at keeping things spic and span. Right? Because God describes the poet and soldier by saying, "I have found that David ... is a man after my Own heart, who will carry out all My wishes." (Acts 13:22 ISV) So King David must have been perfect. Right? If you believe that, we have some swampland in Florida we'd like to sell you. Check out 1st and 2nd Samuel, and try to remember you're not reading *Peyton Place!*

Good Housekeeping

If you've struggled with bad habits or just plain stinking thinking, and you've tried to clean up your act all by your lonesome, then you probably already know how hard it is. Usually, it takes help. And if we want to really come clean, then we need *God's* help! To paraphrase the old ad slogan for Tide laundry detergent, God gets out the dirt others leave behind. But we must first humble ourselves and ask the Creator to clean us up, from the inside out.

"God is faithful and reliable. If we confess our sins, he forgives them and cleanses us from everything we've done wrong." (1 John 1:9 GOD'S WORD)

David realized God's good "housekeeping" starts at the *heart* of things. So he earnestly prayed, "Create in me a clean heart, O God (and) renew a loyal spirit within me. (Psalm 51:10 NLT) David is essentially asking God to help him keep his heart (which is Christ's home, as well as Hospitality HQ) spic and span! But again, we have to *want* a pure heart just as David did.

None of us can accomplish anything until we're good and ready: until we make up our minds, and fully commit ourselves to whatever it takes. Until then, our efforts will be halfhearted and will inevitably fail. This goes for everything from dieting to exercising to quitting smoking. Want a heart that's spic and span? Are you ready to let God commence "spring" cleaning?

So how do we initiate and maintain God's spring cleaning within our hearts? Well, how does one go about keeping the kitchen clean?

First, we have to be committed and engaged in the process: a kitchen doesn't scrub itself! Even "self-cleaning" ovens require that we push the right buttons! Every day we habitually take the proper steps to keep it clean: among other jobs, we wash the dishes, wipe the counters, launder the dish towels, and throw out the trash. These steps ensure that our kitchens are clean and healthy environments (for the preparation of the meals we lovingly serve our "angels"). And a clean kitchen also creates an inviting, welcoming place (where guests will gravitate).

In the same way we habitually take steps to ensure a clean kitchen, the *heart* of the home, we must develop important spiritual habits which keep our hearts clean and properly functioning (to create an inviting, welcoming life that yields edifying fruit!) A clean heart is a hospitable heart!

Walk into your kitchen and look around. Is anything stained or soiled? Anything amiss or out of place? Cracked, chipped or broken? Cluttered and unorganized? David took the same approach to his life. He daily examined his heart, his attitudes and actions, and then asked God to help him in all things and in every area of his life. David was wholly dependent on God!

Jesus said, "I am the vine, you are the branches; he who abides [or remains] in Me and I in him, he bears much fruit, for apart from Me you can do nothing." (John 15:5 NASB)

"Abiding" in God means being humbly and wholly dependent upon Him. Our own efforts are generally pretty pathetic anyway. But God declares that if we remain with Him, confidently relying on His strength and abilities, we will bear "much fruit"! Understand that whenever you rely on your own strength, you actually accomplish *nothing* of eternal spiritual value. That goes for any endeavor, including the practice of hospitality: without the help of the Lord (through the guidance of the Holy Spirit) to keep you balanced, you'll eventually stumble into the pitfalls of entertaining: striving, perfectionism, perhaps even competition and materialism!

This is a good time to point out a simple truth: your efforts at hospitality will have greater impact, and be of far more lasting value, when you trust God *more* than your own abilities at the art of entertaining.

Abiding in God also means keeping Him as your first love and your #1 Priority! It means giving God first place in every area of your life; staying closely connected and in constant communication with Him (through prayer); and always plugged into the source of your strength. You can stay connected to the divine "power supply" by reading, studying and meditating on God's Holy Word. After all, the Bible is the Creator's guide to navigating through life. It's also His special instruction manual to the practice of hospitality, explaining the intricacies of love, peace, acceptance, giving, serving, unity and relationships—the essence of the sacred practice! Learning the "secrets" of God's heart through His "love letter" to us, allows us to understand *who* He is, and *what* He likes and dislikes— along with His wonderful promises, and what He expects from each of us.

You can also stay plugged in by sharing *your* deepest thoughts with God in prayer: your secret hopes and dreams, your struggles and fears, and your love and admiration for Him. Prayer is simply talking honestly to your Creator; and He's listening—all the time!

So, when it comes to keeping our hearts clean and welcoming to both Christ and others, we need to develop the habit of abiding in God, by staying connected and in constant contact with Him, and by keeping our priorities straight. Abiding, furthermore, is just like the practice of hospitality: it should be a family affair, a shared sacred duty within the home of every believer.

Once you've invited Christ into your heart (which then becomes His home and base of operations), you then become a part of *His* spiritual family. Ask your Heavenly *Father* to keep your heart spic and span. Don't resist Him when He finds a spot in your life requiring extra elbow grease, or decides it's time to throw out some of the junk that's cluttering your heart. Remain with Him as He cleans the "kitchen" to make it more hospitable to guests. Abide with Him by spending quality time in daily devotion. Be the branches to His vine, part of an inseparable tangle of wood, which beautifully illustrates how we can each become a part of God, lifting *His* fruit from the soil.

As His "branches," you can become His extended arms—giving, serving, loving—sharing His fruit with a world in need! You can become His angel of hospitality, to your family first, and then to the "stranger"; and *YES!*—you *are* up to this holy charge, because you "...Can do all things through Christ who gives [you] strength." (Philippians 4:13 Berean SB)

There's No Place Like Home!

A clean heart, like a spic and span kitchen, creates an inviting "base of operations" which facilitates hospitality. And a clean heart begins and ends with prayer: first, when you *ask* God to give you a clean heart and a steadfast spirit; second, as you abide in Him by staying in constant *communication* with the Creator; and third, as you *ask* for His guidance and follow His lead in all things. You cannot have the heart of an angel without prayer. Nor can you truly fulfill the call to be hospitable without it!

Prayer is to hospitality what planning and preparation are to the art of entertaining: absolutely essential! Through prayer we receive the Godly wisdom and strength vital to accomplishing our ongoing angelic mission. At the same time, through prayer we avoid the pitfalls of modern entertaining. Prayer is the secret weapon that makes our Mission Possible!

We all know "the best laid plans of mice and men" have a tendency to fail. That's life. But that's why prayer is essential to the practice of hospitality. Even in the best of circumstances, there will always be things that are out of our control. For instance: you plan a cookout—and it rains! You schedule a party for a certain time—and half the guests arrive late! You prepare a special dinner because you want to fuss a little over your company—but at the last minute they cancel on you! It's enough to make a preacher cuss! But instead, you pray!

Or, things can go as planned—sort of—but your guests arrive at the door with their excess emotional baggage in hand: heavy hearts, negative attitudes, grouchy and defensive spirits. *Sigh!* But hey, extending hospitality is about the people, not the plans. It's about ministering to their special needs. So, you keep your peace and go with the flow. But to do this, you'll need to be "prayed up."

Daily prayer will strengthen your connection to the "Prince of Peace," and help prepare you for those aggravating little surprises which will inevitably (and frequently) come your way. Spending time in prayer, especially prior to extending hospitality, also gives your Heavenly Father the opportunity to provide you with direction.

Trust us, He's interested in every detail involved in the sacred practice, from who you invite to what you serve. He'll put specific people in your heart, and give you excellent ideas as to what and how to serve them. He'll make you sensitive to their emotional and spiritual needs, and then show you new ways you can reach them. He'll even help you stretch your budget!

Prayer is important to the success of any endeavor, but it's absolutely indispensable when extending hospitality. It can instill in us the genuine heart of an angel, and then guide and protect that loving and hospitable heart. And prayer, like charity and the practice of hospitality itself, begins in the home! But then, *everything* good begins in the home!

The clean and abiding heart of an angel is like a spotless kitchen: an inviting and welcoming base of operations for giving, serving and ministering. Like the kitchen, this heart for hospitality is actually what makes a house a home. Remember, "Home is where the heart is!" And the "beat" of your hospitable heart should set the entire rhythm of your home!

Father Abraham's heart overflowed with his concern for the needs of three traveling strangers who turned out be angels (of the supernatural variety). And his hospitality to the angels makes him our Biblical icon for the sacred practice! But an even greater truth is found at the *heart* of Abraham's story: his hospitality began in the safe harbor of his own home. The patriarch thus set the pattern for the sacred practice.

The Biblical Martha followed his example when she hosted Jesus Christ in *her* home. And on both a spiritual and a physical level, we're also to follow the examples set by Abraham and Martha, by hosting God in our hearts, and His "angels" in our homes.

Be it ever so humble, there's no place like home! And yet, the home is one of the most underrated and underutilized venues—not only for the practice of hospitality, but also for healing, evangelism, and even miracles!

God wants us to use our homes as sanctuaries for the weary, as oases of refreshing for those going through "dry spells," as mini-hospitals of emotional and spiritual healing for those who are hurting. Our "patients" begin with our families but should ultimately include any angels God sends our way. For it's in the loving and secure environment of the home that our patients are more willing to share their pain and problems, their sorrows and shortcomings.

People feel they can be more transparent in the atmosphere of a loving home. Masks come off, and the secrets of the heart come out. The importance of this can't be overemphasized—not in a world where believers too often deny the reality of their problems and feelings, choosing instead to hide behind an almost robotic façade while mechanically spouting, "I am blessed. I am in total victory." We're called to "share each other's burdens." (Galatians 6:2 NLT) Doing this brings unity and promotes healing, only these days no one's sharing! Fellowship in a loving home can help change this.

In a hospitable home, Koinónia fellowship (honest, open, heart to heart, spirit to spirit communication) can create an atmosphere of love and acceptance, where walls are broken through, bridges are built, hearts mended, and relationships established, nurtured and strengthened—and where true bonding takes place.

The hospitable home is also the perfect place to share the Good News of Jesus Christ. Many people, for various reasons, seem to be turned off by organized religion and the traditional church environment. For many of these people, their shadows will never darken the doors of a house of worship. But these same spiritually needy folk will quickly and gladly accept an invitation to the home of a believer, for a delicious meal and some good social interaction.

Once in the hospitable home of a follower of Christ, they have an opportunity to observe the love of God in action. And the host or hostess has the perfect opportunity to share what the Lord has done in their lives! Hence, the home can become the ultimate mission field.

But again, prayer is the key. Hospitality can be an incredible tool for evangelism when we ask God to guide us in our efforts, to anoint our conversation, and to open a special door through which we can freely share the Gospel about our loving, accepting and welcoming God!

As for miracles, many pastors often state the greatest miracle is salvation itself: when our Heavenly Father supernaturally changes a flawed human being into a right-standing, *new creation*. We agree totally! We've had the privilege of witnessing this miracle in our own home, and when you prayerfully commit the use of your home to God for His hospitable purposes, you can too!

We've stated we're all angels. We all have a message to share. The believer's message is his or her testimony of a changed life! The spiritual journey leading to faith in the Lord and eternal salvation is a story that never gets old. And there's no better place to tell it than in the warmth of your home, in the midst of genuine hospitality—where the host has no agenda other than offering the love of God.

From the Heart of God

We'd like to share one last thing with you, straight from the heart of God. It begins with a wonderful story of His love: about a man who had the heart of an angel. He was a third-century Christian who was martyred for his faith, and we're sure you're familiar with him. In fact, many of you celebrate his lifestyle of love and giving every 14th of February—on Saint Valentine's Day!

The Roman emperor Claudius II had passed a law forbidding Christian worship. Breaking this law was punishable by death, but a man named Valentinus refused to stop following and practicing the teachings of Jesus Christ. So he was arrested and given a death sentence. While imprisoned and awaiting for his sentence to be carried out, Valentinus found favor with his jailer. Realizing that Valentinus was a man of learning, the jailer asked the Christian if he would tutor his daughter, Julia, who had been blind since birth. Valentinus quickly agreed and soon discovered his pretty young pupil had a sharp mind. He read her stories, taught her arithmetic, and told her about his God.

Julia was able to see the world through the eyes of Valentinus. She trusted in his wisdom and found comfort for her blindness in the man's quiet strength. One day she asked Valentinus, "Does God really hear our prayers?"

"Yes, my child," replied Valentinus, "He hears each one."

Julia then explained how she prayed for sight every morning, asking Valentinus if he believed God would answer her prayers. He replied, "God does what is best for us if we only believe in Him."

On that day, Julia knelt and grasped her tutor's hands. Together they prayed, and Julia accepted Christ as her Lord and Savior. Legend teaches that at that moment a brilliant light flooded the tiny prison cell, and Julia received her sight! A happy ending? For Julia, yes; but the story's ultimate ending is bittersweet. Late one evening, Saint Valentinus wrote Julia a letter, urging her to stay close to God. He signed it "from Your Valentine." The next morning, on February 14, 270 A.D., he was taken from prison to his place of execution, a spot now called Porta Valentini in his honor. He was buried at what is today the Church of Praxedes in Rome.

According to legend, Julia often visited his grave, and nearby she planted a pink-blossomed almond tree. Today, the almond tree remains a symbol of abiding love and friendship! And Saint Valentine's Day remains the holiday most associated with love. But we can also commemorate it as a special day of hospitality!

We should be hospitable every single day, of course, but the history surrounding Saint Valentine's Day perfectly illustrates the sacred practice as it relates to Godly love. Remember, hospitality is: God's love expressed in a practical way; it's becoming His hands extended to a hurting, lonely, and lost world, regardless of our resources or circumstances.

Valentinus managed to extend hospitality from the dreary prison cell that had become his home, with nothing more to offer than his love and a listening ear. He gave Julia an opportunity to share her story, and then encouraged her with his own message of the faithfulness of Christ. By being hospitable, Valentinus opened the door to a fruitful relationship with a young woman who needed nothing short of a miracle. Through his *hospitality*, she got one! Along with *another* relationship, which changed her life, a relationship with the Hospitable God of the Bible!

Love is all Valentinus had to offer. But that was okay, because *everything* worthwhile begins and ends with love! It defines the heart of an angel. And it's the foundation of God's sacred practice of hospitality.

The Apostle John writes, "We know how much God loves us, and we have put our trust in His love. God is love, and all who live in love live in God, and God lives in them." (1 John 4:16 NLT) God's true identity is love! Love shapes His character and motivates all His deeds. So, everything the Lord *has done* for us, *is doing* for us, and *will do* for us—was, is, and will be solely out of His infinite love for us!

God is the loving Father who gave us "His one and only Son, so that everyone who believes in Him will not perish but have eternal life." (John 3:16 NLT) He did this "to adopt us into His own family by bringing us to Himself through Jesus Christ. This is what He wanted to do, and it gave Him great pleasure." (Ephesians 1:5 NLT) In essence, our Heavenly Father—in an amazing act of hospitality—made room for us in His home (His Kingdom) and then invited each of us to be a part of His spiritual family!

John 3:16 is probably the most quoted verse of the Bible, because it beautifully illustrates God's hospitable heart! In some translations, such as the King James Version, the word *everyone* is rendered as "whosoever"! Note how inclusive God is: "whosoever" leaves no one out, regardless of their social status, economic or education level, ethnicity, or any other distinction. There are no "strangers" to God's hospitality, because He knows we *all* need a Savior: "...For all have sinned and fall short of the glory of God...." (Romans 3:23 ESV)

God, however, never reduces us to the lowly state of a beggar. Nor does He require us to work for our "portion." To the contrary, His hospitality is cheerfully and freely extended! Paul writes, "God saved you through <u>faith</u> as an act of kindness. You had nothing to do with it. Being saved is a gift from God." (Ephesians 2:8 GOD'S WORD) Nope, we can't brag about our social connections; they carry no weight when God makes out His Heavenly "guest list"!

Are you on God's list? When you believe in the redemptive work of Christ, and trust your salvation to Him (the elements of "faith"), you will be saved! At that moment, your heart is also transformed: Paul writes, "This means that anyone who belongs to Christ has become a new person. The old life is gone; a new life has begun!" (2 Corinthians 5:17 NLT) Wow, come as you are, eat for free, take your place with the family! That's the ultimate in hospitality!

But doesn't God deserve to get something out of all this? Well, He doesn't expect anything—not even a "hostess gift"; but we *can show* our appreciation, and actions always speak louder than words! Which is why, a mere three verses after Paul mentions our "new life," he writes "Therefore, we are ambassadors for Christ." (2 Corinthians 5:17 ESV)

Paul is reminding us that once we become a part of the royal family of God, we also become His representatives regarding all His policies and practices. Representing God means representing who He is, as well as what He does. Since God is love, we must become ambassadors of love. And, since He's the God of Hospitality, we must become ambassadors of His sacred practice, too. But hey, shouldn't we be willing to extend to others a little of the love and hospitality God heaped upon us?

Oh gosh, we hate to say we told you so, but ... HOSPITALITY IS EVERYONE'S RESPONSIBILITY!

Let's review the definition of hospitality: an attitude of the heart (LOVE) expressed through a lifestyle of giving and serving. It's not a series of carefully planned activities scheduled at the convenience of the host, generally during holidays, as in modern entertaining (a secular pursuit). Instead, hospitality is a lifestyle you live out 24 hours a day—365 days a year—whether it's convenient or not.

It's the giving of your time, talents, and resources; but more importantly, it's the giving of yourself. Unlike the art of entertaining, hospitality is concerned with much more than meeting a social obligation or just having a good time. God's sacred practice has a higher purpose: touching lives, mending hearts, building relationships ... and gathering with the "angels"!

The hospitable God of the Bible, more than anything else, desires that we become more like Him. For this reason, Paul admonishes us, "Don't copy the behavior and customs of this world, but let God transform you into a new person by changing the way you think. Then you will learn to know God's will for you, which is good and pleasing and perfect." (Romans 12:2 NLT)

Our Heavenly Father is the essence of love and generosity, giving and sacrifice, selflessness and servanthood. HE IS THE SPIRIT OF HOSPITALITY! If we are to become like Him—to develop the heart of an angel—and fully represent Him, we must become, *first* and *foremost*, GOD'S HOSPITABLE PEOPLE. Indeed, we will never be more like Him than when we're reaching out to those around us in a genuine spirit of Biblical Hospitality.

Dear reader, we truly believe that many of our greatest spiritual, emotional and social ills can be addressed and "cured"—not through the impersonal laws of men practiced in the public arena, but rather by God's Law of Love, expressed through the practice of hospitality, in our homes, across our kitchen tables. Because something supernatural happens when we sit down together to break bread in a spirit of brotherhood and unity: God shows up!

Jesus stated, "Where two or three have come together in my name, I am there among them." (Matthew 18:20 GOD'S WORD) This is certainly true of faith communities, but it also applies to the home! Why not? Home is where the heart is, the starting point for hospitable expressions of God's love that bring people together. *And there's no place like home!*

Open your home to all the wonderful possibilities. When God shows up in the midst of your gatherings, amazing and miraculous things will happen in much the same way as when Jesus visited Martha, or three strangers called on Abraham, or the Angel Gabriel appeared to the Virgin Mary, proclaiming, "...Nothing is impossible with God." (Luke 1:37 NLT)

Open your *heart* to God and your *home* to the angels. Become a Heavenly Messenger of hospitality. Let your family, your friends, and this world in need, know that YOU have the heart of an angel!

—❤—

Additional copies of *The Heart of an Angel*, along with Tom & Wilma's other inspirational books, *Diet for Dreamers* and *Angel in the Kitchen*, may be purchased at: AMAZON.com, BN.com, or BOOKSaMILLION.com

SUPPLEMENT:
GOD'S *SUPERNATURAL* MESSENGERS

In our website and book series we frequently draw an analogy between God's *human* servants and messengers and the supernatural beings known as angels. To avoid any possible confusion, and because there's a good deal of misinformation regarding angels in the media, we offer the following supplemental material.

Hollywood has caused most of the confusion surrounding angels. Big-budget movies depict God's celestial agents in a highly entertaining fashion; but which is rarely Biblically correct. We mentioned, in Chapter 1, the television series *Touched by an Angel*, a show which accurately portrays the hospitable heart of these supernatural emissaries. In general, the show's writers and producers were respectful of their source material (the Bible); but they took some artistic license regarding a major characteristic of angels: gender!

Here are three important Biblical facts about angels:

1. ALL of the angels recorded in the Bible are depicted as males. For several examples, refer to:

   - Genesis 18:1-2; 19:1
   - Daniel 10:12-13, 21; 12:1; and Revelation 12:7
   - Luke 1:26; 24:4-6; and Mark 16:5

2. Angels are spirit beings created distinct from humans. Please refer to:

- Hebrews 1:14; Luke 20:36; 24:39; Ephesians 6:12; Colossians 1:16; Psalm 8:4-5; 148:2-4; 1 Corinthians 15:40

- God separately creates people (man and woman) in Genesis 1:26-31; 2:18-24

3. When humans die, they do NOT turn into angels, who must then "earn their wings"! (Remember the character of Clarence in *It's a Wonderful Life?* Although we truly enjoy this classic Hollywood movie every year at Christmastime, we view it only as a work of total fantasy.) Please refer to:

- Hebrews 9:27; Ecclesiastes 3:2; Psalm 19:9; Romans 14:10; 2 Corinthians 5:10; and Matthew 19:14

- Regarding the Good News of salvation and eternal life through Jesus Christ: "It is all so wonderful that even the angels are eagerly watching these things happen." (1 Peter 1:12 NLT)

- "You know that we will rule angels [when we enter into Heaven]...?" (1 Corinthians 6:3 NIV)

4. Here are 3 excellent resources for further reading:

- *Angels: God's Secret Agents* by Billy Graham (1995: Hodder & Stoughton)

- *Those Invisible Spirits Called Angels* by Renald E. Showers (1997: Friends of Israel Gospel Ministry, Inc.)

- *Angels, Satan, and Demons* by Robert Paul Lightner (2010: IFL Publishing House)

ENDNOTES

THE FEASTS OF THE LORD: RESOURCES

The Feasts of the Lord, discussed in Chapter 5, are initially mentioned in Leviticus 23:1-2. Below are three excellent resources for further reading:

1. *Touching the Heart of God* by Paul Wilbur (2015: Certa Books)

2. *The Feasts of Israel: Seasons of the Messiah* by Bruce Scott (1997: Friends of Israel Gospel Ministry, Inc.)

3. *The Outpouring: Jesus in the Feasts of Israel* by Elwood McQuaid (1990: Friends of Israel Gospel Ministry, Inc.)

DAVID ONELIO ESPAILLAT: HISTORICAL & BIOGRAPHICAL NOTE

Wilma's formative years growing up in the Big Apple were generally idyllic. If you've seen the New York depicted in the movie *You've Got Mail*, you'll have a good idea of the friendly city she fondly remembers. Within this cordial world Wilma caught the hospitality bug at a very early age—after being exposed to the practice by both of her parents.

However, before anyone conjures up images of the "perfect" upbringing, à la *Father Knows Best*; or the "perfect" home, like a picturesque Hispanic version of the *Leave It to Beaver* household, Wilma wishes to set the record straight. Hers is a long and interesting story, but we'll share only a few of the more fascinating facts.

Her father, David Onelio Espaillat Campos, got involved with the Communist Party in the late 1950s. He left New York to return to his native Dominican Republic, where he became one of the key leaders of the MPD (Movimiento Popular Dominicano) and participated in an attempt to overthrow the government there. The attempt might have succeeded—with the Dominican Republic becoming another "Cuba"—if not for the intervention of the United States.

David was eventually captured and imprisoned. But his intentions had always been honorable. Although he was led astray by the false promises of Communism, his goals and actions were in support of freeing his country from what he saw as an oppressive dictatorship. Which is why he is today considered a national hero.

On October 3, 2013 the government of the Dominican Republic commemorated the 30th Anniversary of his death by erecting a Burial Monument in his honor. Wilma's *Papi* also made the history books! Google it sometime.

Of course, when all this was happening, the Espaillat family was at a loss for words. In fact, throughout Wilma's public school and college years, her Papi's involvement with the Communist Party was a dark and closely guarded family secret—for obvious reasons! It was also the cause of more than a little doubt and stress.

Wilma may not have had what actor Tom Hanks jokingly describes in *You've Got Mail* as "just your typical American family"; and her childhood circumstances were far from ideal, but with the help of her Mamita, a steadfast follower of Christ, Wilma nevertheless developed the hospitable heart of an angel. Because of this, she knows you can, too!

OTHER RESOURCES SITED:

Improving Your Serve by Charles R. Swindoll (2004: Thomas Nelson, Inc.)

Jewish Culture and Customs: A Sampler of Jewish Life by Steve Herzig (1997: Friends of Israel Gospel Ministry, Inc.)

Jewish Literacy: The Most Important Things to Know About the Jewish Religion, Its People, and Its History by Rabbi Joseph Telushkin (2008: William Morrow)

My Heart—Christ's Home by Robert Boyd Munger (1986: Intervarsity Press)

The Rituals of Dinner: The Origins, Evolution, Eccentricities, and Meaning of Table Manners by Margaret Visser (2012: HarperCollins)

Webster's 1828 American Dictionary of the English Language (2015: Waking Lion Press)

Made in the USA
Middletown, DE
05 June 2018